THIS BOOK BELONGS TO:

CONTACT INFORMATION	
NAME:	
ADDRESS:	
PHONE:	

START / END DATES

_____ / ___ / ___   TO   _____ / ___ / ___

DEDICATION

This Taco Log Book is dedicated to all the taco enthusiasts out there who want to record all the tacos they have tasted and document their findings in the process.

You are my inspiration for producing books and I'm honored to be a part of keeping all of your taco tasting notes and records organized.

This journal notebook will help you record the details of your taco reviews.

Thoughtfully put together with these sections to record: Taco Shop, Taco Type, Notes, Toppings, Tortilla, Meat, Salsa, Spice Level and much more!

HOW TO USE THIS BOOK

The purpose of this book is to keep all of your Taco Review notes all in one place. It will help keep you organized.

This Taco Log will allow you to accurately document every detail about your taco tastings.

Here are examples of the prompts for you to fill in and write about your experience in this book:

1. Date
2. Taco Shop
3. Location
4. Taco Type
5. Cost
6. Notes
7. Cuisine
8. Toppings
9. Tortilla
10. Meat
11. Salsa Type
12. Spice Level
13. Service
14. Would You Go Back?
15. Overall Rating

TACO LOGBOOK

DATE			○ DINE-IN	○ STREET
TACO SHOP				
LOCATION		COST	$	
TACO TYPE				

NOTES	CUISINE	
	○ MEXICAN	○ FUSION
	○ TEX-MEX	○ OTHER

TOPPINGS				TORTILLA	
○ RICE	○ TOMATO	○ AVOCADO	○ CORN	○ FLOUR	○ CORN
○ BEANS	○ ONION	○ CARROT	○ EGG	○ SOFT	○ HARD
○ CHEESE	○ CILANTRO	○ RADISH	○ OLIVE	○ OTHER	
○ LETTUCE	○ JALAPEÑO	○ CUCUMBER	○ MANGO		
○ CABBAGE	○ BELL PEPPER	○ POTATO	○ LIME	○ HANDMADE	○ PRE-PACKAGED

OTHER	MEAT

SALSA TYPE			SPICE LEVEL				
○ PICO DE GALLO	○ VERDE	○ ROJA	○ 1	○ 2	○ 3	○ 4	○ 5
○ JALAPEÑO	○ GUACAMOLE	○ GUAJILLO	SERVICE				
○ CHIPOTLE	○ TAQUERIA STYLE	○ OTHER	○ 1	○ 2	○ 3	○ 4	○ 5

WOULD YOU GO BACK?		OVERALL RATING
○ YES	○ NO	/ 10

TACO LOGBOOK

DATE		○ DINE-IN	○ STREET
TACO SHOP			
LOCATION		COST	$
TACO TYPE			

NOTES	CUISINE	
	○ MEXICAN	○ FUSION
	○ TEX-MEX	○ OTHER

TOPPINGS				TORTILLA	
○ RICE	○ TOMATO	○ AVOCADO	○ CORN	○ FLOUR	○ CORN
○ BEANS	○ ONION	○ CARROT	○ EGG	○ SOFT	○ HARD
○ CHEESE	○ CILANTRO	○ RADISH	○ OLIVE	○ OTHER	
○ LETTUCE	○ JALAPEÑO	○ CUCUMBER	○ MANGO		
○ CABBAGE	○ BELL PEPPER	○ POTATO	○ LIME	○ HANDMADE	○ PRE-PACKAGED

OTHER	MEAT

SALSA TYPE			SPICE LEVEL				
○ PICO DE GALLO	○ VERDE	○ ROJA	○ 1	○ 2	○ 3	○ 4	○ 5
○ JALAPEÑO	○ GUACAMOLE	○ GUAJILLO	SERVICE				
○ CHIPOTLE	○ TAQUERIA STYLE	○ OTHER	○ 1	○ 2	○ 3	○ 4	○ 5

WOULD YOU GO BACK?		OVERALL RATING
○ YES	○ NO	/ 10

TACO LOGBOOK

DATE			○ DINE-IN	○ STREET
TACO SHOP				
LOCATION		COST	$	
TACO TYPE				

NOTES	CUISINE	
	○ MEXICAN	○ FUSION
	○ TEX-MEX	○ OTHER

TOPPINGS				TORTILLA	
○ RICE	○ TOMATO	○ AVOCADO	○ CORN	○ FLOUR	○ CORN
○ BEANS	○ ONION	○ CARROT	○ EGG	○ SOFT	○ HARD
○ CHEESE	○ CILANTRO	○ RADISH	○ OLIVE	○ OTHER	
○ LETTUCE	○ JALAPEÑO	○ CUCUMBER	○ MANGO		
○ CABBAGE	○ BELL PEPPER	○ POTATO	○ LIME	○ HANDMADE	○ PRE-PACKAGED

OTHER	MEAT

SALSA TYPE			SPICE LEVEL				
○ PICO DE GALLO	○ VERDE	○ ROJA	○ 1	○ 2	○ 3	○ 4	○ 5
○ JALAPEÑO	○ GUACAMOLE	○ GUAJILLO	SERVICE				
○ CHIPOTLE	○ TAQUERIA STYLE	○ OTHER	○ 1	○ 2	○ 3	○ 4	○ 5

WOULD YOU GO BACK?		OVERALL RATING
○ YES	○ NO	/ 10

TACO LOGBOOK

DATE		○ DINE-IN	○ STREET
TACO SHOP			
LOCATION		COST	$
TACO TYPE			

NOTES	CUISINE	
	○ MEXICAN	○ FUSION
	○ TEX-MEX	○ OTHER

TOPPINGS				TORTILLA	
○ RICE	○ TOMATO	○ AVOCADO	○ CORN	○ FLOUR	○ CORN
○ BEANS	○ ONION	○ CARROT	○ EGG	○ SOFT	○ HARD
○ CHEESE	○ CILANTRO	○ RADISH	○ OLIVE	○ OTHER	
○ LETTUCE	○ JALAPEÑO	○ CUCUMBER	○ MANGO		
○ CABBAGE	○ BELL PEPPER	○ POTATO	○ LIME	○ HANDMADE	○ PRE-PACKAGED

OTHER	MEAT

SALSA TYPE			SPICE LEVEL				
○ PICO DE GALLO	○ VERDE	○ ROJA	○ 1	○ 2	○ 3	○ 4	○ 5
○ JALAPEÑO	○ GUACAMOLE	○ GUAJILLO	SERVICE				
○ CHIPOTLE	○ TAQUERIA STYLE	○ OTHER	○ 1	○ 2	○ 3	○ 4	○ 5

WOULD YOU GO BACK?		OVERALL RATING
○ YES	○ NO	/ 10

TACO LOGBOOK

DATE			○ DINE-IN	○ STREET
TACO SHOP				
LOCATION		COST	$	
TACO TYPE				

NOTES	CUISINE	
	○ MEXICAN	○ FUSION
	○ TEX-MEX	○ OTHER

TOPPINGS				TORTILLA	
○ RICE	○ TOMATO	○ AVOCADO	○ CORN	○ FLOUR	○ CORN
○ BEANS	○ ONION	○ CARROT	○ EGG	○ SOFT	○ HARD
○ CHEESE	○ CILANTRO	○ RADISH	○ OLIVE	○ OTHER	
○ LETTUCE	○ JALAPEÑO	○ CUCUMBER	○ MANGO		
○ CABBAGE	○ BELL PEPPER	○ POTATO	○ LIME	○ HANDMADE	○ PRE-PACKAGED

OTHER	MEAT

SALSA TYPE			SPICE LEVEL				
○ PICO DE GALLO	○ VERDE	○ ROJA	○ 1	○ 2	○ 3	○ 4	○ 5
○ JALAPEÑO	○ GUACAMOLE	○ GUAJILLO	SERVICE				
○ CHIPOTLE	○ TAQUERIA STYLE	○ OTHER	○ 1	○ 2	○ 3	○ 4	○ 5

WOULD YOU GO BACK?		OVERALL RATING
○ YES	○ NO	/ 10

TACO LOGBOOK

DATE			○ DINE-IN	○ STREET
TACO SHOP				
LOCATION			COST	$
TACO TYPE				

NOTES	CUISINE	
	○ MEXICAN	○ FUSION
	○ TEX-MEX	○ OTHER

TOPPINGS				TORTILLA	
○ RICE	○ TOMATO	○ AVOCADO	○ CORN	○ FLOUR	○ CORN
○ BEANS	○ ONION	○ CARROT	○ EGG	○ SOFT	○ HARD
○ CHEESE	○ CILANTRO	○ RADISH	○ OLIVE	○ OTHER	
○ LETTUCE	○ JALAPEÑO	○ CUCUMBER	○ MANGO		
○ CABBAGE	○ BELL PEPPER	○ POTATO	○ LIME	○ HANDMADE	○ PRE-PACKAGED

OTHER	MEAT

SALSA TYPE			SPICE LEVEL				
○ PICO DE GALLO	○ VERDE	○ ROJA	○ 1	○ 2	○ 3	○ 4	○ 5
○ JALAPEÑO	○ GUACAMOLE	○ GUAJILLO	SERVICE				
○ CHIPOTLE	○ TAQUERIA STYLE	○ OTHER	○ 1	○ 2	○ 3	○ 4	○ 5

WOULD YOU GO BACK?		OVERALL RATING
○ YES	○ NO	/ 10

TACO LOGBOOK

DATE			○ DINE-IN	○ STREET
TACO SHOP				
LOCATION		COST	$	
TACO TYPE				

NOTES	CUISINE	
	○ MEXICAN	○ FUSION
	○ TEX-MEX	○ OTHER

TOPPINGS				TORTILLA	
○ RICE	○ TOMATO	○ AVOCADO	○ CORN	○ FLOUR	○ CORN
○ BEANS	○ ONION	○ CARROT	○ EGG	○ SOFT	○ HARD
○ CHEESE	○ CILANTRO	○ RADISH	○ OLIVE	○ OTHER	
○ LETTUCE	○ JALAPEÑO	○ CUCUMBER	○ MANGO		
○ CABBAGE	○ BELL PEPPER	○ POTATO	○ LIME	○ HANDMADE	○ PRE-PACKAGED

OTHER	MEAT

SALSA TYPE			SPICE LEVEL				
○ PICO DE GALLO	○ VERDE	○ ROJA	○ 1	○ 2	○ 3	○ 4	○ 5
○ JALAPEÑO	○ GUACAMOLE	○ GUAJILLO	SERVICE				
○ CHIPOTLE	○ TAQUERIA STYLE	○ OTHER	○ 1	○ 2	○ 3	○ 4	○ 5

WOULD YOU GO BACK?		OVERALL RATING
○ YES	○ NO	/ 10

TACO LOGBOOK

DATE		○ DINE-IN	○ STREET
TACO SHOP			
LOCATION		COST $	
TACO TYPE			

NOTES

CUISINE

○ MEXICAN   ○ FUSION
○ TEX-MEX   ○ OTHER

TOPPINGS

○ RICE	○ TOMATO	○ AVOCADO	○ CORN
○ BEANS	○ ONION	○ CARROT	○ EGG
○ CHEESE	○ CILANTRO	○ RADISH	○ OLIVE
○ LETTUCE	○ JALAPEÑO	○ CUCUMBER	○ MANGO
○ CABBAGE	○ BELL PEPPER	○ POTATO	○ LIME

TORTILLA

○ FLOUR	○ CORN
○ SOFT	○ HARD
○ OTHER	
○ HAND-MADE	○ PRE-PACKAGED

OTHER

MEAT

SALSA TYPE

○ PICO DE GALLO	○ VERDE	○ ROJA
○ JALAPEÑO	○ GUACAMOLE	○ GUAJILLO
○ CHIPOTLE	○ TAQUERIA STYLE	○ OTHER

SPICE LEVEL

○ 1   ○ 2   ○ 3   ○ 4   ○ 5

SERVICE

○ 1   ○ 2   ○ 3   ○ 4   ○ 5

WOULD YOU GO BACK?

○ YES   ○ NO

OVERALL RATING

/ 10

TACO LOGBOOK

DATE			○ DINE-IN	○ STREET
TACO SHOP				
LOCATION		COST	$	
TACO TYPE				

NOTES	CUISINE	
	○ MEXICAN	○ FUSION
	○ TEX-MEX	○ OTHER

TOPPINGS				TORTILLA	
○ RICE	○ TOMATO	○ AVOCADO	○ CORN	○ FLOUR	○ CORN
○ BEANS	○ ONION	○ CARROT	○ EGG	○ SOFT	○ HARD
○ CHEESE	○ CILANTRO	○ RADISH	○ OLIVE	○ OTHER	
○ LETTUCE	○ JALAPEÑO	○ CUCUMBER	○ MANGO		
○ CABBAGE	○ BELL PEPPER	○ POTATO	○ LIME	○ HANDMADE	○ PRE-PACKAGED

OTHER	MEAT

SALSA TYPE			SPICE LEVEL				
○ PICO DE GALLO	○ VERDE	○ ROJA	○ 1	○ 2	○ 3	○ 4	○ 5
○ JALAPEÑO	○ GUACAMOLE	○ GUAJILLO	SERVICE				
○ CHIPOTLE	○ TAQUERIA STYLE	○ OTHER	○ 1	○ 2	○ 3	○ 4	○ 5

WOULD YOU GO BACK?		OVERALL RATING
○ YES	○ NO	/ 10

TACO LOGBOOK

DATE		○ DINE-IN	○ STREET
TACO SHOP			
LOCATION		COST	$
TACO TYPE			

NOTES	CUISINE	
	○ MEXICAN	○ FUSION
	○ TEX-MEX	○ OTHER

TOPPINGS				TORTILLA	
○ RICE	○ TOMATO	○ AVOCADO	○ CORN	○ FLOUR	○ CORN
○ BEANS	○ ONION	○ CARROT	○ EGG	○ SOFT	○ HARD
○ CHEESE	○ CILANTRO	○ RADISH	○ OLIVE	○ OTHER	
○ LETTUCE	○ JALAPEÑO	○ CUCUMBER	○ MANGO		
○ CABBAGE	○ BELL PEPPER	○ POTATO	○ LIME	○ HANDMADE	○ PRE-PACKAGED

OTHER	MEAT

SALSA TYPE			SPICE LEVEL				
○ PICO DE GALLO	○ VERDE	○ ROJA	○ 1	○ 2	○ 3	○ 4	○ 5
○ JALAPEÑO	○ GUACAMOLE	○ GUAJILLO	SERVICE				
○ CHIPOTLE	○ TAQUERIA STYLE	○ OTHER	○ 1	○ 2	○ 3	○ 4	○ 5

WOULD YOU GO BACK?		OVERALL RATING
○ YES	○ NO	/ 10

TACO LOGBOOK

DATE			○ DINE-IN	○ STREET
TACO SHOP				
LOCATION			COST	$
TACO TYPE				

NOTES	CUISINE	
	○ MEXICAN	○ FUSION
	○ TEX-MEX	○ OTHER

TOPPINGS				TORTILLA	
○ RICE	○ TOMATO	○ AVOCADO	○ CORN	○ FLOUR	○ CORN
○ BEANS	○ ONION	○ CARROT	○ EGG	○ SOFT	○ HARD
○ CHEESE	○ CILANTRO	○ RADISH	○ OLIVE	○ OTHER	
○ LETTUCE	○ JALAPEÑO	○ CUCUMBER	○ MANGO		
○ CABBAGE	○ BELL PEPPER	○ POTATO	○ LIME	○ HANDMADE	○ PRE-PACKAGED

OTHER	MEAT

SALSA TYPE			SPICE LEVEL				
○ PICO DE GALLO	○ VERDE	○ ROJA	○ 1	○ 2	○ 3	○ 4	○ 5
○ JALAPEÑO	○ GUACAMOLE	○ GUAJILLO	SERVICE				
○ CHIPOTLE	○ TAQUERIA STYLE	○ OTHER	○ 1	○ 2	○ 3	○ 4	○ 5

WOULD YOU GO BACK?		OVERALL RATING
○ YES	○ NO	/ 10

TACO LOGBOOK

DATE			○ DINE-IN	○ STREET
TACO SHOP				
LOCATION		COST	$	
TACO TYPE				

NOTES	CUISINE	
	○ MEXICAN	○ FUSION
	○ TEX-MEX	○ OTHER

TOPPINGS				TORTILLA	
○ RICE	○ TOMATO	○ AVOCADO	○ CORN	○ FLOUR	○ CORN
○ BEANS	○ ONION	○ CARROT	○ EGG	○ SOFT	○ HARD
○ CHEESE	○ CILANTRO	○ RADISH	○ OLIVE	○ OTHER	
○ LETTUCE	○ JALAPEÑO	○ CUCUMBER	○ MANGO		
○ CABBAGE	○ BELL PEPPER	○ POTATO	○ LIME	○ HANDMADE	○ PRE-PACKAGED

OTHER	MEAT

SALSA TYPE			SPICE LEVEL				
○ PICO DE GALLO	○ VERDE	○ ROJA	○ 1	○ 2	○ 3	○ 4	○ 5
○ JALAPEÑO	○ GUACAMOLE	○ GUAJILLO	SERVICE				
○ CHIPOTLE	○ TAQUERIA STYLE	○ OTHER	○ 1	○ 2	○ 3	○ 4	○ 5

WOULD YOU GO BACK?		OVERALL RATING
○ YES	○ NO	/ 10

TACO LOGBOOK

DATE			○ DINE-IN	○ STREET
TACO SHOP				
LOCATION		COST	$	
TACO TYPE				

NOTES	CUISINE	
	○ MEXICAN	○ FUSION
	○ TEX-MEX	○ OTHER

TOPPINGS				TORTILLA	
○ RICE	○ TOMATO	○ AVOCADO	○ CORN	○ FLOUR	○ CORN
○ BEANS	○ ONION	○ CARROT	○ EGG	○ SOFT	○ HARD
○ CHEESE	○ CILANTRO	○ RADISH	○ OLIVE	○ OTHER	
○ LETTUCE	○ JALAPEÑO	○ CUCUMBER	○ MANGO		
○ CABBAGE	○ BELL PEPPER	○ POTATO	○ LIME	○ HANDMADE	○ PRE-PACKAGED

OTHER	MEAT

SALSA TYPE			SPICE LEVEL				
○ PICO DE GALLO	○ VERDE	○ ROJA	○ 1	○ 2	○ 3	○ 4	○ 5
○ JALAPEÑO	○ GUACAMOLE	○ GUAJILLO	SERVICE				
○ CHIPOTLE	○ TAQUERIA STYLE	○ OTHER	○ 1	○ 2	○ 3	○ 4	○ 5

WOULD YOU GO BACK?		OVERALL RATING
○ YES	○ NO	/ 10

TACO LOGBOOK

DATE			○ DINE-IN	○ STREET
TACO SHOP				
LOCATION		COST	$	
TACO TYPE				

NOTES	CUISINE	
	○ MEXICAN	○ FUSION
	○ TEX-MEX	○ OTHER

TOPPINGS				TORTILLA	
○ RICE	○ TOMATO	○ AVOCADO	○ CORN	○ FLOUR	○ CORN
○ BEANS	○ ONION	○ CARROT	○ EGG	○ SOFT	○ HARD
○ CHEESE	○ CILANTRO	○ RADISH	○ OLIVE	○ OTHER	
○ LETTUCE	○ JALAPEÑO	○ CUCUMBER	○ MANGO		
○ CABBAGE	○ BELL PEPPER	○ POTATO	○ LIME	○ HANDMADE	○ PRE-PACKAGED

OTHER	MEAT

SALSA TYPE			SPICE LEVEL				
○ PICO DE GALLO	○ VERDE	○ ROJA	○ 1	○ 2	○ 3	○ 4	○ 5
○ JALAPEÑO	○ GUACAMOLE	○ GUAJILLO	SERVICE				
○ CHIPOTLE	○ TAQUERIA STYLE	○ OTHER	○ 1	○ 2	○ 3	○ 4	○ 5

WOULD YOU GO BACK?		OVERALL RATING
○ YES	○ NO	/ 10

TACO LOGBOOK

DATE			○ DINE-IN	○ STREET
TACO SHOP				
LOCATION		COST	$	
TACO TYPE				

NOTES	CUISINE	
	○ MEXICAN	○ FUSION
	○ TEX-MEX	○ OTHER

TOPPINGS				TORTILLA	
○ RICE	○ TOMATO	○ AVOCADO	○ CORN	○ FLOUR	○ CORN
○ BEANS	○ ONION	○ CARROT	○ EGG	○ SOFT	○ HARD
○ CHEESE	○ CILANTRO	○ RADISH	○ OLIVE	○ OTHER	
○ LETTUCE	○ JALAPEÑO	○ CUCUMBER	○ MANGO		
○ CABBAGE	○ BELL PEPPER	○ POTATO	○ LIME	○ HANDMADE	○ PRE-PACKAGED

OTHER	MEAT

SALSA TYPE			SPICE LEVEL				
○ PICO DE GALLO	○ VERDE	○ ROJA	○ 1	○ 2	○ 3	○ 4	○ 5
○ JALAPEÑO	○ GUACAMOLE	○ GUAJILLO	SERVICE				
○ CHIPOTLE	○ TAQUERIA STYLE	○ OTHER	○ 1	○ 2	○ 3	○ 4	○ 5

WOULD YOU GO BACK?		OVERALL RATING
○ YES	○ NO	/ 10

TACO LOGBOOK

DATE			○ DINE-IN	○ STREET
TACO SHOP				
LOCATION		COST	$	
TACO TYPE				

NOTES	CUISINE	
	○ MEXICAN	○ FUSION
	○ TEX-MEX	○ OTHER

TOPPINGS				TORTILLA	
○ RICE	○ TOMATO	○ AVOCADO	○ CORN	○ FLOUR	○ CORN
○ BEANS	○ ONION	○ CARROT	○ EGG	○ SOFT	○ HARD
○ CHEESE	○ CILANTRO	○ RADISH	○ OLIVE	○ OTHER	
○ LETTUCE	○ JALAPEÑO	○ CUCUMBER	○ MANGO		
○ CABBAGE	○ BELL PEPPER	○ POTATO	○ LIME	○ HANDMADE	○ PRE-PACKAGED

OTHER	MEAT

SALSA TYPE			SPICE LEVEL				
○ PICO DE GALLO	○ VERDE	○ ROJA	○ 1	○ 2	○ 3	○ 4	○ 5
○ JALAPEÑO	○ GUACAMOLE	○ GUAJILLO	SERVICE				
○ CHIPOTLE	○ TAQUERIA STYLE	○ OTHER	○ 1	○ 2	○ 3	○ 4	○ 5

WOULD YOU GO BACK?		OVERALL RATING
○ YES	○ NO	/ 10

TACO LOGBOOK

DATE			○ DINE-IN	○ STREET
TACO SHOP				
LOCATION		COST	$	
TACO TYPE				

NOTES	CUISINE	
	○ MEXICAN	○ FUSION
	○ TEX-MEX	○ OTHER

TOPPINGS				TORTILLA	
○ RICE	○ TOMATO	○ AVOCADO	○ CORN	○ FLOUR	○ CORN
○ BEANS	○ ONION	○ CARROT	○ EGG	○ SOFT	○ HARD
○ CHEESE	○ CILANTRO	○ RADISH	○ OLIVE	○ OTHER	
○ LETTUCE	○ JALAPEÑO	○ CUCUMBER	○ MANGO		
○ CABBAGE	○ BELL PEPPER	○ POTATO	○ LIME	○ HANDMADE	○ PRE-PACKAGED

OTHER	MEAT

SALSA TYPE			SPICE LEVEL				
○ PICO DE GALLO	○ VERDE	○ ROJA	○ 1	○ 2	○ 3	○ 4	○ 5
○ JALAPEÑO	○ GUACAMOLE	○ GUAJILLO	SERVICE				
○ CHIPOTLE	○ TAQUERIA STYLE	○ OTHER	○ 1	○ 2	○ 3	○ 4	○ 5

WOULD YOU GO BACK?		OVERALL RATING
○ YES	○ NO	/ 10

TACO LOGBOOK

DATE			○ DINE-IN	○ STREET
TACO SHOP				
LOCATION		COST	$	
TACO TYPE				

NOTES	CUISINE	
	○ MEXICAN	○ FUSION
	○ TEX-MEX	○ OTHER

TOPPINGS				TORTILLA	
○ RICE	○ TOMATO	○ AVOCADO	○ CORN	○ FLOUR	○ CORN
○ BEANS	○ ONION	○ CARROT	○ EGG	○ SOFT	○ HARD
○ CHEESE	○ CILANTRO	○ RADISH	○ OLIVE	○ OTHER	
○ LETTUCE	○ JALAPEÑO	○ CUCUMBER	○ MANGO		
○ CABBAGE	○ BELL PEPPER	○ POTATO	○ LIME	○ HANDMADE	○ PRE-PACKAGED

OTHER	MEAT

SALSA TYPE			SPICE LEVEL				
○ PICO DE GALLO	○ VERDE	○ ROJA	○ 1	○ 2	○ 3	○ 4	○ 5
○ JALAPEÑO	○ GUACAMOLE	○ GUAJILLO	SERVICE				
○ CHIPOTLE	○ TAQUERIA STYLE	○ OTHER	○ 1	○ 2	○ 3	○ 4	○ 5

WOULD YOU GO BACK?		OVERALL RATING
○ YES	○ NO	/ 10

TACO LOGBOOK

DATE			○ DINE-IN	○ STREET
TACO SHOP				
LOCATION		COST	$	
TACO TYPE				

NOTES	CUISINE
	○ MEXICAN ○ FUSION
	○ TEX-MEX ○ OTHER

TOPPINGS				TORTILLA	
○ RICE	○ TOMATO	○ AVOCADO	○ CORN	○ FLOUR	○ CORN
○ BEANS	○ ONION	○ CARROT	○ EGG	○ SOFT	○ HARD
○ CHEESE	○ CILANTRO	○ RADISH	○ OLIVE	○ OTHER	
○ LETTUCE	○ JALAPEÑO	○ CUCUMBER	○ MANGO		
○ CABBAGE	○ BELL PEPPER	○ POTATO	○ LIME	○ HANDMADE	○ PRE-PACKAGED

OTHER	MEAT

SALSA TYPE			SPICE LEVEL				
○ PICO DE GALLO	○ VERDE	○ ROJA	○ 1	○ 2	○ 3	○ 4	○ 5
○ JALAPEÑO	○ GUACAMOLE	○ GUAJILLO	SERVICE				
○ CHIPOTLE	○ TAQUERIA STYLE	○ OTHER	○ 1	○ 2	○ 3	○ 4	○ 5

WOULD YOU GO BACK?		OVERALL RATING
○ YES	○ NO	/ 10

TACO LOGBOOK

DATE			○ DINE-IN	○ STREET
TACO SHOP				
LOCATION			COST	$
TACO TYPE				

NOTES		CUISINE	
		○ MEXICAN	○ FUSION
		○ TEX-MEX	○ OTHER

TOPPINGS				TORTILLA	
○ RICE	○ TOMATO	○ AVOCADO	○ CORN	○ FLOUR	○ CORN
○ BEANS	○ ONION	○ CARROT	○ EGG	○ SOFT	○ HARD
○ CHEESE	○ CILANTRO	○ RADISH	○ OLIVE	○ OTHER	
○ LETTUCE	○ JALAPEÑO	○ CUCUMBER	○ MANGO		
○ CABBAGE	○ BELL PEPPER	○ POTATO	○ LIME	○ HANDMADE	○ PRE-PACKAGED

OTHER	MEAT

SALSA TYPE			SPICE LEVEL				
○ PICO DE GALLO	○ VERDE	○ ROJA	○ 1	○ 2	○ 3	○ 4	○ 5
○ JALAPEÑO	○ GUACAMOLE	○ GUAJILLO	SERVICE				
○ CHIPOTLE	○ TAQUERIA STYLE	○ OTHER	○ 1	○ 2	○ 3	○ 4	○ 5

WOULD YOU GO BACK?		OVERALL RATING
○ YES	○ NO	/ 10

TACO LOGBOOK

DATE		○ DINE-IN	○ STREET
TACO SHOP			
LOCATION		COST	$
TACO TYPE			

NOTES	CUISINE	
	○ MEXICAN	○ FUSION
	○ TEX-MEX	○ OTHER

TOPPINGS				TORTILLA	
○ RICE	○ TOMATO	○ AVOCADO	○ CORN	○ FLOUR	○ CORN
○ BEANS	○ ONION	○ CARROT	○ EGG	○ SOFT	○ HARD
○ CHEESE	○ CILANTRO	○ RADISH	○ OLIVE	○ OTHER	
○ LETTUCE	○ JALAPEÑO	○ CUCUMBER	○ MANGO		
○ CABBAGE	○ BELL PEPPER	○ POTATO	○ LIME	○ HANDMADE	○ PRE-PACKAGED

OTHER	MEAT

SALSA TYPE			SPICE LEVEL				
○ PICO DE GALLO	○ VERDE	○ ROJA	○ 1	○ 2	○ 3	○ 4	○ 5
○ JALAPEÑO	○ GUACAMOLE	○ GUAJILLO	SERVICE				
○ CHIPOTLE	○ TAQUERIA STYLE	○ OTHER	○ 1	○ 2	○ 3	○ 4	○ 5

WOULD YOU GO BACK?		OVERALL RATING
○ YES	○ NO	/ 10

TACO LOGBOOK

DATE		○ DINE-IN	○ STREET
TACO SHOP			
LOCATION		COST	$
TACO TYPE			

NOTES	CUISINE	
	○ MEXICAN	○ FUSION
	○ TEX-MEX	○ OTHER

TOPPINGS				TORTILLA	
○ RICE	○ TOMATO	○ AVOCADO	○ CORN	○ FLOUR	○ CORN
○ BEANS	○ ONION	○ CARROT	○ EGG	○ SOFT	○ HARD
○ CHEESE	○ CILANTRO	○ RADISH	○ OLIVE	○ OTHER	
○ LETTUCE	○ JALAPEÑO	○ CUCUMBER	○ MANGO		
○ CABBAGE	○ BELL PEPPER	○ POTATO	○ LIME	○ HANDMADE	○ PRE-PACKAGED

OTHER	MEAT

SALSA TYPE			SPICE LEVEL				
○ PICO DE GALLO	○ VERDE	○ ROJA	○ 1	○ 2	○ 3	○ 4	○ 5
○ JALAPEÑO	○ GUACAMOLE	○ GUAJILLO	SERVICE				
○ CHIPOTLE	○ TAQUERIA STYLE	○ OTHER	○ 1	○ 2	○ 3	○ 4	○ 5

WOULD YOU GO BACK?		OVERALL RATING
○ YES	○ NO	/ 10

TACO LOGBOOK

DATE				○ DINE-IN	○ STREET
TACO SHOP					
LOCATION			COST	$	
TACO TYPE					

NOTES		CUISINE	
		○ MEXICAN	○ FUSION
		○ TEX-MEX	○ OTHER

TOPPINGS				TORTILLA	
○ RICE	○ TOMATO	○ AVOCADO	○ CORN	○ FLOUR	○ CORN
○ BEANS	○ ONION	○ CARROT	○ EGG	○ SOFT	○ HARD
○ CHEESE	○ CILANTRO	○ RADISH	○ OLIVE	○ OTHER	
○ LETTUCE	○ JALAPEÑO	○ CUCUMBER	○ MANGO		
○ CABBAGE	○ BELL PEPPER	○ POTATO	○ LIME	○ HANDMADE	○ PRE-PACKAGED

OTHER	MEAT

SALSA TYPE			SPICE LEVEL				
○ PICO DE GALLO	○ VERDE	○ ROJA	○ 1	○ 2	○ 3	○ 4	○ 5
○ JALAPEÑO	○ GUACAMOLE	○ GUAJILLO	SERVICE				
○ CHIPOTLE	○ TAQUERIA STYLE	○ OTHER	○ 1	○ 2	○ 3	○ 4	○ 5

WOULD YOU GO BACK?		OVERALL RATING
○ YES	○ NO	/ 10

TACO LOGBOOK

DATE		○ DINE-IN	○ STREET
TACO SHOP			
LOCATION		COST	$
TACO TYPE			

NOTES	CUISINE	
	○ MEXICAN	○ FUSION
	○ TEX-MEX	○ OTHER

TOPPINGS

					TORTILLA	
○ RICE	○ TOMATO	○ AVOCADO	○ CORN	○ FLOUR		○ CORN
○ BEANS	○ ONION	○ CARROT	○ EGG	○ SOFT		○ HARD
○ CHEESE	○ CILANTRO	○ RADISH	○ OLIVE	○ OTHER		
○ LETTUCE	○ JALAPEÑO	○ CUCUMBER	○ MANGO			
○ CABBAGE	○ BELL PEPPER	○ POTATO	○ LIME	○ HANDMADE		○ PRE-PACKAGED

OTHER / MEAT

OTHER	MEAT

SALSA TYPE / SPICE LEVEL

			SPICE LEVEL				
○ PICO DE GALLO	○ VERDE	○ ROJA	○ 1	○ 2	○ 3	○ 4	○ 5
○ JALAPEÑO	○ GUACAMOLE	○ GUAJILLO	SERVICE				
○ CHIPOTLE	○ TAQUERIA STYLE	○ OTHER	○ 1	○ 2	○ 3	○ 4	○ 5

WOULD YOU GO BACK?	OVERALL RATING
○ YES ○ NO	/ 10

TACO LOGBOOK

DATE			○ DINE-IN	○ STREET
TACO SHOP				
LOCATION		COST	$	
TACO TYPE				

NOTES	CUISINE	
	○ MEXICAN	○ FUSION
	○ TEX-MEX	○ OTHER

TOPPINGS				TORTILLA	
○ RICE	○ TOMATO	○ AVOCADO	○ CORN	○ FLOUR	○ CORN
○ BEANS	○ ONION	○ CARROT	○ EGG	○ SOFT	○ HARD
○ CHEESE	○ CILANTRO	○ RADISH	○ OLIVE	○ OTHER	
○ LETTUCE	○ JALAPEÑO	○ CUCUMBER	○ MANGO		
○ CABBAGE	○ BELL PEPPER	○ POTATO	○ LIME	○ HANDMADE	○ PRE-PACKAGED

OTHER	MEAT

SALSA TYPE			SPICE LEVEL				
○ PICO DE GALLO	○ VERDE	○ ROJA	○ 1	○ 2	○ 3	○ 4	○ 5
○ JALAPEÑO	○ GUACAMOLE	○ GUAJILLO	SERVICE				
○ CHIPOTLE	○ TAQUERIA STYLE	○ OTHER	○ 1	○ 2	○ 3	○ 4	○ 5

WOULD YOU GO BACK?		OVERALL RATING
○ YES	○ NO	/ 10

TACO LOGBOOK

DATE			○ DINE-IN	○ STREET
TACO SHOP				
LOCATION		COST	$	
TACO TYPE				

NOTES	CUISINE	
	○ MEXICAN	○ FUSION
	○ TEX-MEX	○ OTHER

TOPPINGS				TORTILLA	
○ RICE	○ TOMATO	○ AVOCADO	○ CORN	○ FLOUR	○ CORN
○ BEANS	○ ONION	○ CARROT	○ EGG	○ SOFT	○ HARD
○ CHEESE	○ CILANTRO	○ RADISH	○ OLIVE	○ OTHER	
○ LETTUCE	○ JALAPEÑO	○ CUCUMBER	○ MANGO		
○ CABBAGE	○ BELL PEPPER	○ POTATO	○ LIME	○ HANDMADE	○ PRE-PACKAGED

OTHER	MEAT

SALSA TYPE			SPICE LEVEL				
○ PICO DE GALLO	○ VERDE	○ ROJA	○ 1	○ 2	○ 3	○ 4	○ 5
○ JALAPEÑO	○ GUACAMOLE	○ GUAJILLO	SERVICE				
○ CHIPOTLE	○ TAQUERIA STYLE	○ OTHER	○ 1	○ 2	○ 3	○ 4	○ 5

WOULD YOU GO BACK?		OVERALL RATING
○ YES	○ NO	/ 10

TACO LOGBOOK

DATE			○ DINE-IN	○ STREET
TACO SHOP				
LOCATION		COST	$	
TACO TYPE				

NOTES	CUISINE	
	○ MEXICAN	○ FUSION
	○ TEX-MEX	○ OTHER

TOPPINGS				TORTILLA	
○ RICE	○ TOMATO	○ AVOCADO	○ CORN	○ FLOUR	○ CORN
○ BEANS	○ ONION	○ CARROT	○ EGG	○ SOFT	○ HARD
○ CHEESE	○ CILANTRO	○ RADISH	○ OLIVE	○ OTHER	
○ LETTUCE	○ JALAPEÑO	○ CUCUMBER	○ MANGO		
○ CABBAGE	○ BELL PEPPER	○ POTATO	○ LIME	○ HANDMADE	○ PRE-PACKAGED

OTHER	MEAT

SALSA TYPE			SPICE LEVEL				
○ PICO DE GALLO	○ VERDE	○ ROJA	○ 1	○ 2	○ 3	○ 4	○ 5
○ JALAPEÑO	○ GUACAMOLE	○ GUAJILLO	SERVICE				
○ CHIPOTLE	○ TAQUERIA STYLE	○ OTHER	○ 1	○ 2	○ 3	○ 4	○ 5

WOULD YOU GO BACK?		OVERALL RATING
○ YES	○ NO	/ 10

TACO LOGBOOK

DATE			○ DINE-IN	○ STREET
TACO SHOP				
LOCATION		COST	$	
TACO TYPE				

NOTES	CUISINE	
	○ MEXICAN	○ FUSION
	○ TEX-MEX	○ OTHER

TOPPINGS				TORTILLA	
○ RICE	○ TOMATO	○ AVOCADO	○ CORN	○ FLOUR	○ CORN
○ BEANS	○ ONION	○ CARROT	○ EGG	○ SOFT	○ HARD
○ CHEESE	○ CILANTRO	○ RADISH	○ OLIVE	○ OTHER	
○ LETTUCE	○ JALAPEÑO	○ CUCUMBER	○ MANGO		
○ CABBAGE	○ BELL PEPPER	○ POTATO	○ LIME	○ HANDMADE	○ PRE-PACKAGED

OTHER	MEAT

SALSA TYPE			SPICE LEVEL				
○ PICO DE GALLO	○ VERDE	○ ROJA	○ 1	○ 2	○ 3	○ 4	○ 5
○ JALAPEÑO	○ GUACAMOLE	○ GUAJILLO	SERVICE				
○ CHIPOTLE	○ TAQUERIA STYLE	○ OTHER	○ 1	○ 2	○ 3	○ 4	○ 5

WOULD YOU GO BACK?		OVERALL RATING
○ YES	○ NO	/ 10

TACO LOGBOOK

DATE			○ DINE-IN	○ STREET
TACO SHOP				
LOCATION		COST	$	
TACO TYPE				

NOTES	CUISINE	
	○ MEXICAN	○ FUSION
	○ TEX-MEX	○ OTHER

TOPPINGS				TORTILLA	
○ RICE	○ TOMATO	○ AVOCADO	○ CORN	○ FLOUR	○ CORN
○ BEANS	○ ONION	○ CARROT	○ EGG	○ SOFT	○ HARD
○ CHEESE	○ CILANTRO	○ RADISH	○ OLIVE	○ OTHER	
○ LETTUCE	○ JALAPEÑO	○ CUCUMBER	○ MANGO		
○ CABBAGE	○ BELL PEPPER	○ POTATO	○ LIME	○ HANDMADE	○ PRE-PACKAGED

OTHER	MEAT

SALSA TYPE			SPICE LEVEL				
○ PICO DE GALLO	○ VERDE	○ ROJA	○ 1	○ 2	○ 3	○ 4	○ 5
○ JALAPEÑO	○ GUACAMOLE	○ GUAJILLO	SERVICE				
○ CHIPOTLE	○ TAQUERIA STYLE	○ OTHER	○ 1	○ 2	○ 3	○ 4	○ 5

WOULD YOU GO BACK?		OVERALL RATING
○ YES	○ NO	/ 10

TACO LOGBOOK

DATE		○ DINE-IN	○ STREET
TACO SHOP			
LOCATION		COST	$
TACO TYPE			

NOTES

CUISINE

○ MEXICAN ○ FUSION
○ TEX-MEX ○ OTHER

TOPPINGS

○ RICE	○ TOMATO	○ AVOCADO	○ CORN
○ BEANS	○ ONION	○ CARROT	○ EGG
○ CHEESE	○ CILANTRO	○ RADISH	○ OLIVE
○ LETTUCE	○ JALAPEÑO	○ CUCUMBER	○ MANGO
○ CABBAGE	○ BELL PEPPER	○ POTATO	○ LIME

TORTILLA

○ FLOUR	○ CORN
○ SOFT	○ HARD
○ OTHER	
○ HANDMADE	○ PRE-PACKAGED

OTHER

MEAT

SALSA TYPE

○ PICO DE GALLO	○ VERDE	○ ROJA
○ JALAPEÑO	○ GUACAMOLE	○ GUAJILLO
○ CHIPOTLE	○ TAQUERIA STYLE	○ OTHER

SPICE LEVEL

○ 1 ○ 2 ○ 3 ○ 4 ○ 5

SERVICE

○ 1 ○ 2 ○ 3 ○ 4 ○ 5

WOULD YOU GO BACK?

○ YES   ○ NO

OVERALL RATING

/ 10

TACO LOGBOOK

DATE			○ DINE-IN	○ STREET
TACO SHOP				
LOCATION		COST	$	
TACO TYPE				

NOTES	CUISINE	
	○ MEXICAN	○ FUSION
	○ TEX-MEX	○ OTHER

TOPPINGS				TORTILLA	
○ RICE	○ TOMATO	○ AVOCADO	○ CORN	○ FLOUR	○ CORN
○ BEANS	○ ONION	○ CARROT	○ EGG	○ SOFT	○ HARD
○ CHEESE	○ CILANTRO	○ RADISH	○ OLIVE	○ OTHER	
○ LETTUCE	○ JALAPEÑO	○ CUCUMBER	○ MANGO		
○ CABBAGE	○ BELL PEPPER	○ POTATO	○ LIME	○ HANDMADE	○ PRE-PACKAGED

OTHER	MEAT

SALSA TYPE			SPICE LEVEL				
○ PICO DE GALLO	○ VERDE	○ ROJA	○ 1	○ 2	○ 3	○ 4	○ 5
○ JALAPEÑO	○ GUACAMOLE	○ GUAJILLO	SERVICE				
○ CHIPOTLE	○ TAQUERIA STYLE	○ OTHER	○ 1	○ 2	○ 3	○ 4	○ 5

WOULD YOU GO BACK?		OVERALL RATING
○ YES	○ NO	/ 10

TACO LOGBOOK

DATE			○ DINE-IN	○ STREET
TACO SHOP				
LOCATION		COST	$	
TACO TYPE				

NOTES	CUISINE	
	○ MEXICAN	○ FUSION
	○ TEX-MEX	○ OTHER

TOPPINGS				TORTILLA	
○ RICE	○ TOMATO	○ AVOCADO	○ CORN	○ FLOUR	○ CORN
○ BEANS	○ ONION	○ CARROT	○ EGG	○ SOFT	○ HARD
○ CHEESE	○ CILANTRO	○ RADISH	○ OLIVE	○ OTHER	
○ LETTUCE	○ JALAPEÑO	○ CUCUMBER	○ MANGO		
○ CABBAGE	○ BELL PEPPER	○ POTATO	○ LIME	○ HANDMADE	○ PRE-PACKAGED

OTHER	MEAT

SALSA TYPE			SPICE LEVEL				
○ PICO DE GALLO	○ VERDE	○ ROJA	○ 1	○ 2	○ 3	○ 4	○ 5
○ JALAPEÑO	○ GUACAMOLE	○ GUAJILLO	SERVICE				
○ CHIPOTLE	○ TAQUERIA STYLE	○ OTHER	○ 1	○ 2	○ 3	○ 4	○ 5

WOULD YOU GO BACK?		OVERALL RATING
○ YES	○ NO	/ 10

TACO LOGBOOK

DATE			○ DINE-IN	○ STREET
TACO SHOP				
LOCATION		COST	$	
TACO TYPE				

NOTES	CUISINE	
	○ MEXICAN	○ FUSION
	○ TEX-MEX	○ OTHER

TOPPINGS				TORTILLA	
○ RICE	○ TOMATO	○ AVOCADO	○ CORN	○ FLOUR	○ CORN
○ BEANS	○ ONION	○ CARROT	○ EGG	○ SOFT	○ HARD
○ CHEESE	○ CILANTRO	○ RADISH	○ OLIVE	○ OTHER	
○ LETTUCE	○ JALAPEÑO	○ CUCUMBER	○ MANGO		
○ CABBAGE	○ BELL PEPPER	○ POTATO	○ LIME	○ HANDMADE	○ PRE-PACKAGED

OTHER	MEAT

SALSA TYPE			SPICE LEVEL				
○ PICO DE GALLO	○ VERDE	○ ROJA	○ 1	○ 2	○ 3	○ 4	○ 5
○ JALAPEÑO	○ GUACAMOLE	○ GUAJILLO	SERVICE				
○ CHIPOTLE	○ TAQUERIA STYLE	○ OTHER	○ 1	○ 2	○ 3	○ 4	○ 5

WOULD YOU GO BACK?		OVERALL RATING
○ YES	○ NO	/ 10

TACO LOGBOOK

DATE			○ DINE-IN	○ STREET
TACO SHOP				
LOCATION			**COST** $	
TACO TYPE				

NOTES		CUISINE	
		○ MEXICAN	○ FUSION
		○ TEX-MEX	○ OTHER

TOPPINGS				TORTILLA	
○ RICE	○ TOMATO	○ AVOCADO	○ CORN	○ FLOUR	○ CORN
○ BEANS	○ ONION	○ CARROT	○ EGG	○ SOFT	○ HARD
○ CHEESE	○ CILANTRO	○ RADISH	○ OLIVE	○ OTHER	
○ LETTUCE	○ JALAPEÑO	○ CUCUMBER	○ MANGO		
○ CABBAGE	○ BELL PEPPER	○ POTATO	○ LIME	○ HANDMADE	○ PRE-PACKAGED

OTHER	MEAT

SALSA TYPE			SPICE LEVEL				
○ PICO DE GALLO	○ VERDE	○ ROJA	○ 1	○ 2	○ 3	○ 4	○ 5
○ JALAPEÑO	○ GUACAMOLE	○ GUAJILLO	SERVICE				
○ CHIPOTLE	○ TAQUERIA STYLE	○ OTHER	○ 1	○ 2	○ 3	○ 4	○ 5

WOULD YOU GO BACK?		OVERALL RATING
○ YES	○ NO	/ 10

TACO LOGBOOK

DATE			○ DINE-IN	○ STREET
TACO SHOP				
LOCATION		COST	$	
TACO TYPE				

NOTES	CUISINE	
	○ MEXICAN	○ FUSION
	○ TEX-MEX	○ OTHER

TOPPINGS				TORTILLA	
○ RICE	○ TOMATO	○ AVOCADO	○ CORN	○ FLOUR	○ CORN
○ BEANS	○ ONION	○ CARROT	○ EGG	○ SOFT	○ HARD
○ CHEESE	○ CILANTRO	○ RADISH	○ OLIVE	○ OTHER	
○ LETTUCE	○ JALAPEÑO	○ CUCUMBER	○ MANGO		
○ CABBAGE	○ BELL PEPPER	○ POTATO	○ LIME	○ HANDMADE	○ PRE-PACKAGED

OTHER	MEAT

SALSA TYPE			SPICE LEVEL				
○ PICO DE GALLO	○ VERDE	○ ROJA	○ 1	○ 2	○ 3	○ 4	○ 5
○ JALAPEÑO	○ GUACAMOLE	○ GUAJILLO	SERVICE				
○ CHIPOTLE	○ TAQUERIA STYLE	○ OTHER	○ 1	○ 2	○ 3	○ 4	○ 5

WOULD YOU GO BACK?		OVERALL RATING
○ YES	○ NO	/ 10

TACO LOGBOOK

DATE			○ DINE-IN	○ STREET
TACO SHOP				
LOCATION		COST	$	
TACO TYPE				

NOTES	CUISINE	
	○ MEXICAN	○ FUSION
	○ TEX-MEX	○ OTHER

TOPPINGS				TORTILLA	
○ RICE	○ TOMATO	○ AVOCADO	○ CORN	○ FLOUR	○ CORN
○ BEANS	○ ONION	○ CARROT	○ EGG	○ SOFT	○ HARD
○ CHEESE	○ CILANTRO	○ RADISH	○ OLIVE	○ OTHER	
○ LETTUCE	○ JALAPEÑO	○ CUCUMBER	○ MANGO		
○ CABBAGE	○ BELL PEPPER	○ POTATO	○ LIME	○ HANDMADE	○ PRE-PACKAGED

OTHER	MEAT

SALSA TYPE			SPICE LEVEL				
○ PICO DE GALLO	○ VERDE	○ ROJA	○ 1	○ 2	○ 3	○ 4	○ 5
○ JALAPEÑO	○ GUACAMOLE	○ GUAJILLO	SERVICE				
○ CHIPOTLE	○ TAQUERIA STYLE	○ OTHER	○ 1	○ 2	○ 3	○ 4	○ 5

WOULD YOU GO BACK?		OVERALL RATING
○ YES	○ NO	/ 10

TACO LOGBOOK

DATE			○ DINE-IN	○ STREET
TACO SHOP				
LOCATION			COST $	
TACO TYPE				

NOTES	CUISINE	
	○ MEXICAN	○ FUSION
	○ TEX-MEX	○ OTHER

TOPPINGS				TORTILLA	
○ RICE	○ TOMATO	○ AVOCADO	○ CORN	○ FLOUR	○ CORN
○ BEANS	○ ONION	○ CARROT	○ EGG	○ SOFT	○ HARD
○ CHEESE	○ CILANTRO	○ RADISH	○ OLIVE	○ OTHER	
○ LETTUCE	○ JALAPEÑO	○ CUCUMBER	○ MANGO		
○ CABBAGE	○ BELL PEPPER	○ POTATO	○ LIME	○ HANDMADE	○ PRE-PACKAGED

OTHER	MEAT

SALSA TYPE			SPICE LEVEL				
○ PICO DE GALLO	○ VERDE	○ ROJA	○ 1	○ 2	○ 3	○ 4	○ 5
○ JALAPEÑO	○ GUACAMOLE	○ GUAJILLO	SERVICE				
○ CHIPOTLE	○ TAQUERIA STYLE	○ OTHER	○ 1	○ 2	○ 3	○ 4	○ 5

WOULD YOU GO BACK?		OVERALL RATING
○ YES	○ NO	/ 10

TACO LOGBOOK

DATE			○ DINE-IN	○ STREET
TACO SHOP				
LOCATION		COST	$	
TACO TYPE				

NOTES	CUISINE	
	○ MEXICAN	○ FUSION
	○ TEX-MEX	○ OTHER

TOPPINGS				TORTILLA	
○ RICE	○ TOMATO	○ AVOCADO	○ CORN	○ FLOUR	○ CORN
○ BEANS	○ ONION	○ CARROT	○ EGG	○ SOFT	○ HARD
○ CHEESE	○ CILANTRO	○ RADISH	○ OLIVE	○ OTHER	
○ LETTUCE	○ JALAPEÑO	○ CUCUMBER	○ MANGO		
○ CABBAGE	○ BELL PEPPER	○ POTATO	○ LIME	○ HANDMADE	○ PRE-PACKAGED

OTHER	MEAT

SALSA TYPE			SPICE LEVEL				
○ PICO DE GALLO	○ VERDE	○ ROJA	○ 1	○ 2	○ 3	○ 4	○ 5
○ JALAPEÑO	○ GUACAMOLE	○ GUAJILLO	SERVICE				
○ CHIPOTLE	○ TAQUERIA STYLE	○ OTHER	○ 1	○ 2	○ 3	○ 4	○ 5

WOULD YOU GO BACK?		OVERALL RATING
○ YES	○ NO	/ 10

TACO LOGBOOK

DATE			○ DINE-IN	○ STREET
TACO SHOP				
LOCATION		COST	$	
TACO TYPE				

NOTES	CUISINE	
	○ MEXICAN	○ FUSION
	○ TEX-MEX	○ OTHER

TOPPINGS				TORTILLA	
○ RICE	○ TOMATO	○ AVOCADO	○ CORN	○ FLOUR	○ CORN
○ BEANS	○ ONION	○ CARROT	○ EGG	○ SOFT	○ HARD
○ CHEESE	○ CILANTRO	○ RADISH	○ OLIVE	○ OTHER	
○ LETTUCE	○ JALAPEÑO	○ CUCUMBER	○ MANGO		
○ CABBAGE	○ BELL PEPPER	○ POTATO	○ LIME	○ HANDMADE	○ PRE-PACKAGED

OTHER	MEAT

SALSA TYPE			SPICE LEVEL				
○ PICO DE GALLO	○ VERDE	○ ROJA	○ 1	○ 2	○ 3	○ 4	○ 5
○ JALAPEÑO	○ GUACAMOLE	○ GUAJILLO	SERVICE				
○ CHIPOTLE	○ TAQUERIA STYLE	○ OTHER	○ 1	○ 2	○ 3	○ 4	○ 5

WOULD YOU GO BACK?		OVERALL RATING
○ YES	○ NO	/ 10

TACO LOGBOOK

DATE			○ DINE-IN	○ STREET
TACO SHOP				
LOCATION		COST	$	
TACO TYPE				

NOTES	CUISINE	
	○ MEXICAN	○ FUSION
	○ TEX-MEX	○ OTHER

TOPPINGS				TORTILLA	
○ RICE	○ TOMATO	○ AVOCADO	○ CORN	○ FLOUR	○ CORN
○ BEANS	○ ONION	○ CARROT	○ EGG	○ SOFT	○ HARD
○ CHEESE	○ CILANTRO	○ RADISH	○ OLIVE	○ OTHER	
○ LETTUCE	○ JALAPEÑO	○ CUCUMBER	○ MANGO		
○ CABBAGE	○ BELL PEPPER	○ POTATO	○ LIME	○ HANDMADE	○ PRE-PACKAGED

OTHER	MEAT

SALSA TYPE			SPICE LEVEL				
○ PICO DE GALLO	○ VERDE	○ ROJA	○ 1	○ 2	○ 3	○ 4	○ 5
○ JALAPEÑO	○ GUACAMOLE	○ GUAJILLO	SERVICE				
○ CHIPOTLE	○ TAQUERIA STYLE	○ OTHER	○ 1	○ 2	○ 3	○ 4	○ 5

WOULD YOU GO BACK?		OVERALL RATING
○ YES	○ NO	/ 10

TACO LOGBOOK

DATE			○ DINE-IN	○ STREET
TACO SHOP				
LOCATION		COST	$	
TACO TYPE				

NOTES	CUISINE	
	○ MEXICAN	○ FUSION
	○ TEX-MEX	○ OTHER

TOPPINGS				TORTILLA	
○ RICE	○ TOMATO	○ AVOCADO	○ CORN	○ FLOUR	○ CORN
○ BEANS	○ ONION	○ CARROT	○ EGG	○ SOFT	○ HARD
○ CHEESE	○ CILANTRO	○ RADISH	○ OLIVE	○ OTHER	
○ LETTUCE	○ JALAPEÑO	○ CUCUMBER	○ MANGO		
○ CABBAGE	○ BELL PEPPER	○ POTATO	○ LIME	○ HANDMADE	○ PRE-PACKAGED

OTHER	MEAT

SALSA TYPE			SPICE LEVEL				
○ PICO DE GALLO	○ VERDE	○ ROJA	○ 1	○ 2	○ 3	○ 4	○ 5
○ JALAPEÑO	○ GUACAMOLE	○ GUAJILLO	SERVICE				
○ CHIPOTLE	○ TAQUERIA STYLE	○ OTHER	○ 1	○ 2	○ 3	○ 4	○ 5

WOULD YOU GO BACK?		OVERALL RATING
○ YES	○ NO	/ 10

TACO LOGBOOK

DATE				○ DINE-IN	○ STREET
TACO SHOP					
LOCATION				COST	$
TACO TYPE					

NOTES

CUISINE

○ MEXICAN ○ FUSION
○ TEX-MEX ○ OTHER

TOPPINGS

○ RICE	○ TOMATO	○ AVOCADO	○ CORN
○ BEANS	○ ONION	○ CARROT	○ EGG
○ CHEESE	○ CILANTRO	○ RADISH	○ OLIVE
○ LETTUCE	○ JALAPEÑO	○ CUCUMBER	○ MANGO
○ CABBAGE	○ BELL PEPPER	○ POTATO	○ LIME

TORTILLA

○ FLOUR	○ CORN
○ SOFT	○ HARD
○ OTHER	
○ HANDMADE	○ PRE-PACKAGED

OTHER

MEAT

SALSA TYPE

○ PICO DE GALLO	○ VERDE	○ ROJA
○ JALAPEÑO	○ GUACAMOLE	○ GUAJILLO
○ CHIPOTLE	○ TAQUERIA STYLE	○ OTHER

SPICE LEVEL

○ 1   ○ 2   ○ 3   ○ 4   ○ 5

SERVICE

○ 1   ○ 2   ○ 3   ○ 4   ○ 5

WOULD YOU GO BACK?

○ YES   ○ NO

OVERALL RATING

/ 10

TACO LOGBOOK

DATE			○ DINE-IN	○ STREET
TACO SHOP				
LOCATION		COST	$	
TACO TYPE				

NOTES	CUISINE	
	○ MEXICAN	○ FUSION
	○ TEX-MEX	○ OTHER

TOPPINGS				TORTILLA	
○ RICE	○ TOMATO	○ AVOCADO	○ CORN	○ FLOUR	○ CORN
○ BEANS	○ ONION	○ CARROT	○ EGG	○ SOFT	○ HARD
○ CHEESE	○ CILANTRO	○ RADISH	○ OLIVE	○ OTHER	
○ LETTUCE	○ JALAPEÑO	○ CUCUMBER	○ MANGO		
○ CABBAGE	○ BELL PEPPER	○ POTATO	○ LIME	○ HANDMADE	○ PRE-PACKAGED

OTHER	MEAT

SALSA TYPE			SPICE LEVEL				
○ PICO DE GALLO	○ VERDE	○ ROJA	○ 1	○ 2	○ 3	○ 4	○ 5
○ JALAPEÑO	○ GUACAMOLE	○ GUAJILLO	SERVICE				
○ CHIPOTLE	○ TAQUERIA STYLE	○ OTHER	○ 1	○ 2	○ 3	○ 4	○ 5

WOULD YOU GO BACK?		OVERALL RATING
○ YES	○ NO	/ 10

TACO LOGBOOK

DATE			○ DINE-IN	○ STREET
TACO SHOP				
LOCATION		COST	$	
TACO TYPE				

NOTES	CUISINE	
	○ MEXICAN	○ FUSION
	○ TEX-MEX	○ OTHER

TOPPINGS				TORTILLA	
○ RICE	○ TOMATO	○ AVOCADO	○ CORN	○ FLOUR	○ CORN
○ BEANS	○ ONION	○ CARROT	○ EGG	○ SOFT	○ HARD
○ CHEESE	○ CILANTRO	○ RADISH	○ OLIVE	○ OTHER	
○ LETTUCE	○ JALAPEÑO	○ CUCUMBER	○ MANGO		
○ CABBAGE	○ BELL PEPPER	○ POTATO	○ LIME	○ HANDMADE	○ PRE-PACKAGED

OTHER	MEAT

SALSA TYPE			SPICE LEVEL				
○ PICO DE GALLO	○ VERDE	○ ROJA	○ 1	○ 2	○ 3	○ 4	○ 5
○ JALAPEÑO	○ GUACAMOLE	○ GUAJILLO	SERVICE				
○ CHIPOTLE	○ TAQUERIA STYLE	○ OTHER	○ 1	○ 2	○ 3	○ 4	○ 5

WOULD YOU GO BACK?		OVERALL RATING
○ YES	○ NO	/ 10

TACO LOGBOOK

DATE			○ DINE-IN	○ STREET
TACO SHOP				
LOCATION			COST	$
TACO TYPE				

NOTES	CUISINE	
	○ MEXICAN	○ FUSION
	○ TEX-MEX	○ OTHER

TOPPINGS				TORTILLA	
○ RICE	○ TOMATO	○ AVOCADO	○ CORN	○ FLOUR	○ CORN
○ BEANS	○ ONION	○ CARROT	○ EGG	○ SOFT	○ HARD
○ CHEESE	○ CILANTRO	○ RADISH	○ OLIVE	○ OTHER	
○ LETTUCE	○ JALAPEÑO	○ CUCUMBER	○ MANGO		
○ CABBAGE	○ BELL PEPPER	○ POTATO	○ LIME	○ HANDMADE	○ PRE-PACKAGED

OTHER	MEAT

SALSA TYPE			SPICE LEVEL				
○ PICO DE GALLO	○ VERDE	○ ROJA	○ 1	○ 2	○ 3	○ 4	○ 5
○ JALAPEÑO	○ GUACAMOLE	○ GUAJILLO	SERVICE				
○ CHIPOTLE	○ TAQUERIA STYLE	○ OTHER	○ 1	○ 2	○ 3	○ 4	○ 5

WOULD YOU GO BACK?		OVERALL RATING
○ YES	○ NO	/ 10

TACO LOGBOOK

DATE			○ DINE-IN	○ STREET
TACO SHOP				
LOCATION		COST	$	
TACO TYPE				

NOTES	CUISINE	
	○ MEXICAN	○ FUSION
	○ TEX-MEX	○ OTHER

TOPPINGS				TORTILLA	
○ RICE	○ TOMATO	○ AVOCADO	○ CORN	○ FLOUR	○ CORN
○ BEANS	○ ONION	○ CARROT	○ EGG	○ SOFT	○ HARD
○ CHEESE	○ CILANTRO	○ RADISH	○ OLIVE	○ OTHER	
○ LETTUCE	○ JALAPEÑO	○ CUCUMBER	○ MANGO		
○ CABBAGE	○ BELL PEPPER	○ POTATO	○ LIME	○ HANDMADE	○ PRE-PACKAGED

OTHER	MEAT

SALSA TYPE			SPICE LEVEL				
○ PICO DE GALLO	○ VERDE	○ ROJA	○ 1	○ 2	○ 3	○ 4	○ 5
○ JALAPEÑO	○ GUACAMOLE	○ GUAJILLO	SERVICE				
○ CHIPOTLE	○ TAQUERIA STYLE	○ OTHER	○ 1	○ 2	○ 3	○ 4	○ 5

WOULD YOU GO BACK?		OVERALL RATING
○ YES	○ NO	/ 10

TACO LOGBOOK

DATE			○ DINE-IN	○ STREET
TACO SHOP				
LOCATION		COST	$	
TACO TYPE				

NOTES	CUISINE	
	○ MEXICAN	○ FUSION
	○ TEX-MEX	○ OTHER

TOPPINGS				TORTILLA	
○ RICE	○ TOMATO	○ AVOCADO	○ CORN	○ FLOUR	○ CORN
○ BEANS	○ ONION	○ CARROT	○ EGG	○ SOFT	○ HARD
○ CHEESE	○ CILANTRO	○ RADISH	○ OLIVE	○ OTHER	
○ LETTUCE	○ JALAPEÑO	○ CUCUMBER	○ MANGO		
○ CABBAGE	○ BELL PEPPER	○ POTATO	○ LIME	○ HANDMADE	○ PRE-PACKAGED

OTHER	MEAT

SALSA TYPE			SPICE LEVEL				
○ PICO DE GALLO	○ VERDE	○ ROJA	○ 1	○ 2	○ 3	○ 4	○ 5
○ JALAPEÑO	○ GUACAMOLE	○ GUAJILLO	SERVICE				
○ CHIPOTLE	○ TAQUERIA STYLE	○ OTHER	○ 1	○ 2	○ 3	○ 4	○ 5

WOULD YOU GO BACK?		OVERALL RATING
○ YES	○ NO	/ 10

TACO LOGBOOK

DATE			○ DINE-IN	○ STREET
TACO SHOP				
LOCATION		COST	$	
TACO TYPE				

NOTES	CUISINE	
	○ MEXICAN	○ FUSION
	○ TEX-MEX	○ OTHER

TOPPINGS				TORTILLA	
○ RICE	○ TOMATO	○ AVOCADO	○ CORN	○ FLOUR	○ CORN
○ BEANS	○ ONION	○ CARROT	○ EGG	○ SOFT	○ HARD
○ CHEESE	○ CILANTRO	○ RADISH	○ OLIVE	○ OTHER	
○ LETTUCE	○ JALAPEÑO	○ CUCUMBER	○ MANGO		
○ CABBAGE	○ BELL PEPPER	○ POTATO	○ LIME	○ HANDMADE	○ PRE-PACKAGED

OTHER	MEAT

SALSA TYPE			SPICE LEVEL				
○ PICO DE GALLO	○ VERDE	○ ROJA	○ 1	○ 2	○ 3	○ 4	○ 5
○ JALAPEÑO	○ GUACAMOLE	○ GUAJILLO	SERVICE				
○ CHIPOTLE	○ TAQUERIA STYLE	○ OTHER	○ 1	○ 2	○ 3	○ 4	○ 5

WOULD YOU GO BACK?		OVERALL RATING
○ YES	○ NO	/ 10

TACO LOGBOOK

DATE			○ DINE-IN	○ STREET
TACO SHOP				
LOCATION		COST	$	
TACO TYPE				

NOTES	CUISINE	
	○ MEXICAN	○ FUSION
	○ TEX-MEX	○ OTHER

TOPPINGS				TORTILLA	
○ RICE	○ TOMATO	○ AVOCADO	○ CORN	○ FLOUR	○ CORN
○ BEANS	○ ONION	○ CARROT	○ EGG	○ SOFT	○ HARD
○ CHEESE	○ CILANTRO	○ RADISH	○ OLIVE	○ OTHER	
○ LETTUCE	○ JALAPEÑO	○ CUCUMBER	○ MANGO		
○ CABBAGE	○ BELL PEPPER	○ POTATO	○ LIME	○ HANDMADE	○ PRE-PACKAGED

OTHER	MEAT

SALSA TYPE			SPICE LEVEL				
○ PICO DE GALLO	○ VERDE	○ ROJA	○ 1	○ 2	○ 3	○ 4	○ 5
○ JALAPEÑO	○ GUACAMOLE	○ GUAJILLO	SERVICE				
○ CHIPOTLE	○ TAQUERIA STYLE	○ OTHER	○ 1	○ 2	○ 3	○ 4	○ 5

WOULD YOU GO BACK?		OVERALL RATING
○ YES	○ NO	/ 10

TACO LOGBOOK

DATE			○ DINE-IN	○ STREET
TACO SHOP				
LOCATION		COST $		
TACO TYPE				

NOTES	CUISINE	
	○ MEXICAN	○ FUSION
	○ TEX-MEX	○ OTHER

TOPPINGS				TORTILLA	
○ RICE	○ TOMATO	○ AVOCADO	○ CORN	○ FLOUR	○ CORN
○ BEANS	○ ONION	○ CARROT	○ EGG	○ SOFT	○ HARD
○ CHEESE	○ CILANTRO	○ RADISH	○ OLIVE	○ OTHER	
○ LETTUCE	○ JALAPEÑO	○ CUCUMBER	○ MANGO		
○ CABBAGE	○ BELL PEPPER	○ POTATO	○ LIME	○ HANDMADE	○ PRE-PACKAGED

OTHER	MEAT

SALSA TYPE			SPICE LEVEL				
○ PICO DE GALLO	○ VERDE	○ ROJA	○ 1	○ 2	○ 3	○ 4	○ 5
○ JALAPEÑO	○ GUACAMOLE	○ GUAJILLO	SERVICE				
○ CHIPOTLE	○ TAQUERIA STYLE	○ OTHER	○ 1	○ 2	○ 3	○ 4	○ 5

WOULD YOU GO BACK?		OVERALL RATING
○ YES	○ NO	/ 10

TACO LOGBOOK

DATE			○ DINE-IN	○ STREET
TACO SHOP				
LOCATION		COST	$	
TACO TYPE				

NOTES	CUISINE	
	○ MEXICAN	○ FUSION
	○ TEX-MEX	○ OTHER

TOPPINGS				TORTILLA	
○ RICE	○ TOMATO	○ AVOCADO	○ CORN	○ FLOUR	○ CORN
○ BEANS	○ ONION	○ CARROT	○ EGG	○ SOFT	○ HARD
○ CHEESE	○ CILANTRO	○ RADISH	○ OLIVE	○ OTHER	
○ LETTUCE	○ JALAPEÑO	○ CUCUMBER	○ MANGO		
○ CABBAGE	○ BELL PEPPER	○ POTATO	○ LIME	○ HANDMADE	○ PRE-PACKAGED

OTHER	MEAT

SALSA TYPE			SPICE LEVEL				
○ PICO DE GALLO	○ VERDE	○ ROJA	○ 1	○ 2	○ 3	○ 4	○ 5
○ JALAPEÑO	○ GUACAMOLE	○ GUAJILLO	SERVICE				
○ CHIPOTLE	○ TAQUERIA STYLE	○ OTHER	○ 1	○ 2	○ 3	○ 4	○ 5

WOULD YOU GO BACK?		OVERALL RATING
○ YES	○ NO	/ 10

TACO LOGBOOK

DATE				○ DINE-IN	○ STREET
TACO SHOP					
LOCATION				COST	$
TACO TYPE					

NOTES		CUISINE	
		○ MEXICAN	○ FUSION
		○ TEX-MEX	○ OTHER

TOPPINGS				TORTILLA	
○ RICE	○ TOMATO	○ AVOCADO	○ CORN	○ FLOUR	○ CORN
○ BEANS	○ ONION	○ CARROT	○ EGG	○ SOFT	○ HARD
○ CHEESE	○ CILANTRO	○ RADISH	○ OLIVE	○ OTHER	
○ LETTUCE	○ JALAPEÑO	○ CUCUMBER	○ MANGO		
○ CABBAGE	○ BELL PEPPER	○ POTATO	○ LIME	○ HANDMADE	○ PRE-PACKAGED

OTHER	MEAT

SALSA TYPE			SPICE LEVEL				
○ PICO DE GALLO	○ VERDE	○ ROJA	○ 1	○ 2	○ 3	○ 4	○ 5
○ JALAPEÑO	○ GUACAMOLE	○ GUAJILLO	SERVICE				
○ CHIPOTLE	○ TAQUERIA STYLE	○ OTHER	○ 1	○ 2	○ 3	○ 4	○ 5

WOULD YOU GO BACK?		OVERALL RATING
○ YES	○ NO	/ 10

TACO LOGBOOK

DATE			○ DINE-IN	○ STREET
TACO SHOP				
LOCATION		COST	$	
TACO TYPE				

NOTES	CUISINE	
	○ MEXICAN	○ FUSION
	○ TEX-MEX	○ OTHER

TOPPINGS				TORTILLA	
○ RICE	○ TOMATO	○ AVOCADO	○ CORN	○ FLOUR	○ CORN
○ BEANS	○ ONION	○ CARROT	○ EGG	○ SOFT	○ HARD
○ CHEESE	○ CILANTRO	○ RADISH	○ OLIVE	○ OTHER	
○ LETTUCE	○ JALAPEÑO	○ CUCUMBER	○ MANGO		
○ CABBAGE	○ BELL PEPPER	○ POTATO	○ LIME	○ HANDMADE	○ PRE-PACKAGED

OTHER	MEAT

SALSA TYPE			SPICE LEVEL				
○ PICO DE GALLO	○ VERDE	○ ROJA	○ 1	○ 2	○ 3	○ 4	○ 5
○ JALAPEÑO	○ GUACAMOLE	○ GUAJILLO	SERVICE				
○ CHIPOTLE	○ TAQUERIA STYLE	○ OTHER	○ 1	○ 2	○ 3	○ 4	○ 5

WOULD YOU GO BACK?		OVERALL RATING
○ YES	○ NO	/ 10

TACO LOGBOOK

DATE				○ DINE-IN	○ STREET
TACO SHOP					
LOCATION				COST	$
TACO TYPE					

NOTES		CUISINE	
		○ MEXICAN	○ FUSION
		○ TEX-MEX	○ OTHER

TOPPINGS				TORTILLA	
○ RICE	○ TOMATO	○ AVOCADO	○ CORN	○ FLOUR	○ CORN
○ BEANS	○ ONION	○ CARROT	○ EGG	○ SOFT	○ HARD
○ CHEESE	○ CILANTRO	○ RADISH	○ OLIVE	○ OTHER	
○ LETTUCE	○ JALAPEÑO	○ CUCUMBER	○ MANGO		
○ CABBAGE	○ BELL PEPPER	○ POTATO	○ LIME	○ HANDMADE	○ PRE-PACKAGED

OTHER	MEAT

SALSA TYPE			SPICE LEVEL				
○ PICO DE GALLO	○ VERDE	○ ROJA	○ 1	○ 2	○ 3	○ 4	○ 5
○ JALAPEÑO	○ GUACAMOLE	○ GUAJILLO	SERVICE				
○ CHIPOTLE	○ TAQUERIA STYLE	○ OTHER	○ 1	○ 2	○ 3	○ 4	○ 5

WOULD YOU GO BACK?		OVERALL RATING
○ YES	○ NO	/ 10

TACO LOGBOOK

DATE			○ DINE-IN	○ STREET
TACO SHOP				
LOCATION		COST $		
TACO TYPE				

NOTES	CUISINE	
	○ MEXICAN	○ FUSION
	○ TEX-MEX	○ OTHER

TOPPINGS				TORTILLA	
○ RICE	○ TOMATO	○ AVOCADO	○ CORN	○ FLOUR	○ CORN
○ BEANS	○ ONION	○ CARROT	○ EGG	○ SOFT	○ HARD
○ CHEESE	○ CILANTRO	○ RADISH	○ OLIVE	○ OTHER	
○ LETTUCE	○ JALAPEÑO	○ CUCUMBER	○ MANGO		
○ CABBAGE	○ BELL PEPPER	○ POTATO	○ LIME	○ HANDMADE	○ PRE-PACKAGED

OTHER	MEAT

SALSA TYPE			SPICE LEVEL				
○ PICO DE GALLO	○ VERDE	○ ROJA	○ 1	○ 2	○ 3	○ 4	○ 5
○ JALAPEÑO	○ GUACAMOLE	○ GUAJILLO	SERVICE				
○ CHIPOTLE	○ TAQUERIA STYLE	○ OTHER	○ 1	○ 2	○ 3	○ 4	○ 5

WOULD YOU GO BACK?		OVERALL RATING
○ YES	○ NO	/ 10

TACO LOGBOOK

DATE				○ DINE-IN	○ STREET
TACO SHOP					
LOCATION			COST	$	
TACO TYPE					

NOTES		CUISINE	
		○ MEXICAN	○ FUSION
		○ TEX-MEX	○ OTHER

TOPPINGS				TORTILLA	
○ RICE	○ TOMATO	○ AVOCADO	○ CORN	○ FLOUR	○ CORN
○ BEANS	○ ONION	○ CARROT	○ EGG	○ SOFT	○ HARD
○ CHEESE	○ CILANTRO	○ RADISH	○ OLIVE	○ OTHER	
○ LETTUCE	○ JALAPEÑO	○ CUCUMBER	○ MANGO		
○ CABBAGE	○ BELL PEPPER	○ POTATO	○ LIME	○ HANDMADE	○ PRE-PACKAGED

OTHER	MEAT

SALSA TYPE			SPICE LEVEL				
○ PICO DE GALLO	○ VERDE	○ ROJA	○ 1	○ 2	○ 3	○ 4	○ 5
○ JALAPEÑO	○ GUACAMOLE	○ GUAJILLO	SERVICE				
○ CHIPOTLE	○ TAQUERIA STYLE	○ OTHER	○ 1	○ 2	○ 3	○ 4	○ 5

WOULD YOU GO BACK?		OVERALL RATING
○ YES	○ NO	/ 10

TACO LOGBOOK

DATE			○ DINE-IN	○ STREET
TACO SHOP				
LOCATION		COST	$	
TACO TYPE				

NOTES	CUISINE	
	○ MEXICAN	○ FUSION
	○ TEX-MEX	○ OTHER

TOPPINGS				TORTILLA	
○ RICE	○ TOMATO	○ AVOCADO	○ CORN	○ FLOUR	○ CORN
○ BEANS	○ ONION	○ CARROT	○ EGG	○ SOFT	○ HARD
○ CHEESE	○ CILANTRO	○ RADISH	○ OLIVE	○ OTHER	
○ LETTUCE	○ JALAPEÑO	○ CUCUMBER	○ MANGO		
○ CABBAGE	○ BELL PEPPER	○ POTATO	○ LIME	○ HANDMADE	○ PRE-PACKAGED

OTHER	MEAT

SALSA TYPE			SPICE LEVEL				
○ PICO DE GALLO	○ VERDE	○ ROJA	○ 1	○ 2	○ 3	○ 4	○ 5
○ JALAPEÑO	○ GUACAMOLE	○ GUAJILLO	SERVICE				
○ CHIPOTLE	○ TAQUERIA STYLE	○ OTHER	○ 1	○ 2	○ 3	○ 4	○ 5

WOULD YOU GO BACK?		OVERALL RATING
○ YES	○ NO	/ 10

TACO LOGBOOK

DATE			○ DINE-IN	○ STREET
TACO SHOP				
LOCATION			COST	$
TACO TYPE				

NOTES	CUISINE	
	○ MEXICAN	○ FUSION
	○ TEX-MEX	○ OTHER

TOPPINGS				TORTILLA	
○ RICE	○ TOMATO	○ AVOCADO	○ CORN	○ FLOUR	○ CORN
○ BEANS	○ ONION	○ CARROT	○ EGG	○ SOFT	○ HARD
○ CHEESE	○ CILANTRO	○ RADISH	○ OLIVE	○ OTHER	
○ LETTUCE	○ JALAPEÑO	○ CUCUMBER	○ MANGO		
○ CABBAGE	○ BELL PEPPER	○ POTATO	○ LIME	○ HANDMADE	○ PRE-PACKAGED

OTHER	MEAT

SALSA TYPE			SPICE LEVEL				
○ PICO DE GALLO	○ VERDE	○ ROJA	○ 1	○ 2	○ 3	○ 4	○ 5
○ JALAPEÑO	○ GUACAMOLE	○ GUAJILLO	SERVICE				
○ CHIPOTLE	○ TAQUERIA STYLE	○ OTHER	○ 1	○ 2	○ 3	○ 4	○ 5

WOULD YOU GO BACK?		OVERALL RATING
○ YES	○ NO	/ 10

TACO LOGBOOK

DATE			○ DINE-IN	○ STREET
TACO SHOP				
LOCATION		COST	$	
TACO TYPE				

NOTES		CUISINE	
		○ MEXICAN	○ FUSION
		○ TEX-MEX	○ OTHER

TOPPINGS				TORTILLA	
○ RICE	○ TOMATO	○ AVOCADO	○ CORN	○ FLOUR	○ CORN
○ BEANS	○ ONION	○ CARROT	○ EGG	○ SOFT	○ HARD
○ CHEESE	○ CILANTRO	○ RADISH	○ OLIVE	○ OTHER	
○ LETTUCE	○ JALAPEÑO	○ CUCUMBER	○ MANGO		
○ CABBAGE	○ BELL PEPPER	○ POTATO	○ LIME	○ HANDMADE	○ PRE-PACKAGED

OTHER	MEAT

SALSA TYPE			SPICE LEVEL				
○ PICO DE GALLO	○ VERDE	○ ROJA	○ 1	○ 2	○ 3	○ 4	○ 5
○ JALAPEÑO	○ GUACAMOLE	○ GUAJILLO	SERVICE				
○ CHIPOTLE	○ TAQUERIA STYLE	○ OTHER	○ 1	○ 2	○ 3	○ 4	○ 5

WOULD YOU GO BACK?		OVERALL RATING
○ YES	○ NO	/ 10

TACO LOGBOOK

DATE				○ DINE-IN	○ STREET
TACO SHOP					
LOCATION				COST	$
TACO TYPE					

NOTES		CUISINE	
		○ MEXICAN	○ FUSION
		○ TEX-MEX	○ OTHER

TOPPINGS				TORTILLA	
○ RICE	○ TOMATO	○ AVOCADO	○ CORN	○ FLOUR	○ CORN
○ BEANS	○ ONION	○ CARROT	○ EGG	○ SOFT	○ HARD
○ CHEESE	○ CILANTRO	○ RADISH	○ OLIVE	○ OTHER	
○ LETTUCE	○ JALAPEÑO	○ CUCUMBER	○ MANGO		
○ CABBAGE	○ BELL PEPPER	○ POTATO	○ LIME	○ HANDMADE	○ PRE-PACKAGED

OTHER	MEAT

SALSA TYPE			SPICE LEVEL				
○ PICO DE GALLO	○ VERDE	○ ROJA	○ 1	○ 2	○ 3	○ 4	○ 5
○ JALAPEÑO	○ GUACAMOLE	○ GUAJILLO	SERVICE				
○ CHIPOTLE	○ TAQUERIA STYLE	○ OTHER	○ 1	○ 2	○ 3	○ 4	○ 5

WOULD YOU GO BACK?		OVERALL RATING
○ YES	○ NO	/ 10

TACO LOGBOOK

DATE			○ DINE-IN	○ STREET
TACO SHOP				
LOCATION		COST	$	
TACO TYPE				

NOTES	CUISINE	
	○ MEXICAN	○ FUSION
	○ TEX-MEX	○ OTHER

TOPPINGS				TORTILLA	
○ RICE	○ TOMATO	○ AVOCADO	○ CORN	○ FLOUR	○ CORN
○ BEANS	○ ONION	○ CARROT	○ EGG	○ SOFT	○ HARD
○ CHEESE	○ CILANTRO	○ RADISH	○ OLIVE	○ OTHER	
○ LETTUCE	○ JALAPEÑO	○ CUCUMBER	○ MANGO		
○ CABBAGE	○ BELL PEPPER	○ POTATO	○ LIME	○ HANDMADE	○ PRE-PACKAGED

OTHER	MEAT

SALSA TYPE			SPICE LEVEL				
○ PICO DE GALLO	○ VERDE	○ ROJA	○ 1	○ 2	○ 3	○ 4	○ 5
○ JALAPEÑO	○ GUACAMOLE	○ GUAJILLO	SERVICE				
○ CHIPOTLE	○ TAQUERIA STYLE	○ OTHER	○ 1	○ 2	○ 3	○ 4	○ 5

WOULD YOU GO BACK?		OVERALL RATING
○ YES	○ NO	/ 10

TACO LOGBOOK

DATE			○ DINE-IN	○ STREET
TACO SHOP				
LOCATION		COST	$	
TACO TYPE				

NOTES		CUISINE	
		○ MEXICAN	○ FUSION
		○ TEX-MEX	○ OTHER

TOPPINGS				TORTILLA	
○ RICE	○ TOMATO	○ AVOCADO	○ CORN	○ FLOUR	○ CORN
○ BEANS	○ ONION	○ CARROT	○ EGG	○ SOFT	○ HARD
○ CHEESE	○ CILANTRO	○ RADISH	○ OLIVE	○ OTHER	
○ LETTUCE	○ JALAPEÑO	○ CUCUMBER	○ MANGO		
○ CABBAGE	○ BELL PEPPER	○ POTATO	○ LIME	○ HANDMADE	○ PRE-PACKAGED

OTHER	MEAT

SALSA TYPE			SPICE LEVEL				
○ PICO DE GALLO	○ VERDE	○ ROJA	○ 1	○ 2	○ 3	○ 4	○ 5
○ JALAPEÑO	○ GUACAMOLE	○ GUAJILLO	SERVICE				
○ CHIPOTLE	○ TAQUERIA STYLE	○ OTHER	○ 1	○ 2	○ 3	○ 4	○ 5

WOULD YOU GO BACK?		OVERALL RATING
○ YES	○ NO	/ 10

TACO LOGBOOK

DATE			○ DINE-IN	○ STREET
TACO SHOP				
LOCATION		COST	$	
TACO TYPE				

NOTES	CUISINE	
	○ MEXICAN	○ FUSION
	○ TEX-MEX	○ OTHER

TOPPINGS				TORTILLA	
○ RICE	○ TOMATO	○ AVOCADO	○ CORN	○ FLOUR	○ CORN
○ BEANS	○ ONION	○ CARROT	○ EGG	○ SOFT	○ HARD
○ CHEESE	○ CILANTRO	○ RADISH	○ OLIVE	○ OTHER	
○ LETTUCE	○ JALAPEÑO	○ CUCUMBER	○ MANGO		
○ CABBAGE	○ BELL PEPPER	○ POTATO	○ LIME	○ HANDMADE	○ PRE-PACKAGED

OTHER	MEAT

SALSA TYPE			SPICE LEVEL				
○ PICO DE GALLO	○ VERDE	○ ROJA	○ 1	○ 2	○ 3	○ 4	○ 5
○ JALAPEÑO	○ GUACAMOLE	○ GUAJILLO	SERVICE				
○ CHIPOTLE	○ TAQUERIA STYLE	○ OTHER	○ 1	○ 2	○ 3	○ 4	○ 5

WOULD YOU GO BACK?		OVERALL RATING
○ YES	○ NO	/ 10

TACO LOGBOOK

DATE				○ DINE-IN	○ STREET
TACO SHOP					
LOCATION				COST	$
TACO TYPE					

NOTES | CUISINE

NOTES		CUISINE	
		○ MEXICAN	○ FUSION
		○ TEX-MEX	○ OTHER

TOPPINGS | TORTILLA

TOPPINGS				TORTILLA	
○ RICE	○ TOMATO	○ AVOCADO	○ CORN	○ FLOUR	○ CORN
○ BEANS	○ ONION	○ CARROT	○ EGG	○ SOFT	○ HARD
○ CHEESE	○ CILANTRO	○ RADISH	○ OLIVE	○ OTHER	
○ LETTUCE	○ JALAPEÑO	○ CUCUMBER	○ MANGO		
○ CABBAGE	○ BELL PEPPER	○ POTATO	○ LIME	○ HANDMADE	○ PRE-PACKAGED

OTHER | MEAT

OTHER	MEAT

SALSA TYPE | SPICE LEVEL

SALSA TYPE			SPICE LEVEL				
○ PICO DE GALLO	○ VERDE	○ ROJA	○ 1	○ 2	○ 3	○ 4	○ 5
○ JALAPEÑO	○ GUACAMOLE	○ GUAJILLO	SERVICE				
○ CHIPOTLE	○ TAQUERIA STYLE	○ OTHER	○ 1	○ 2	○ 3	○ 4	○ 5

WOULD YOU GO BACK? | OVERALL RATING

WOULD YOU GO BACK?		OVERALL RATING
○ YES	○ NO	/ 10

TACO LOGBOOK

DATE			○ DINE-IN	○ STREET
TACO SHOP				
LOCATION		COST	$	
TACO TYPE				

NOTES	CUISINE	
	○ MEXICAN	○ FUSION
	○ TEX-MEX	○ OTHER

TOPPINGS				TORTILLA	
○ RICE	○ TOMATO	○ AVOCADO	○ CORN	○ FLOUR	○ CORN
○ BEANS	○ ONION	○ CARROT	○ EGG	○ SOFT	○ HARD
○ CHEESE	○ CILANTRO	○ RADISH	○ OLIVE	○ OTHER	
○ LETTUCE	○ JALAPEÑO	○ CUCUMBER	○ MANGO		
○ CABBAGE	○ BELL PEPPER	○ POTATO	○ LIME	○ HANDMADE	○ PRE-PACKAGED

OTHER	MEAT

SALSA TYPE			SPICE LEVEL				
○ PICO DE GALLO	○ VERDE	○ ROJA	○ 1	○ 2	○ 3	○ 4	○ 5
○ JALAPEÑO	○ GUACAMOLE	○ GUAJILLO	SERVICE				
○ CHIPOTLE	○ TAQUERIA STYLE	○ OTHER	○ 1	○ 2	○ 3	○ 4	○ 5

WOULD YOU GO BACK?		OVERALL RATING
○ YES	○ NO	/ 10

TACO LOGBOOK

DATE			○ DINE-IN	○ STREET
TACO SHOP				
LOCATION			COST	$
TACO TYPE				

NOTES	CUISINE	
	○ MEXICAN	○ FUSION
	○ TEX-MEX	○ OTHER

TOPPINGS				TORTILLA	
○ RICE	○ TOMATO	○ AVOCADO	○ CORN	○ FLOUR	○ CORN
○ BEANS	○ ONION	○ CARROT	○ EGG	○ SOFT	○ HARD
○ CHEESE	○ CILANTRO	○ RADISH	○ OLIVE	○ OTHER	
○ LETTUCE	○ JALAPEÑO	○ CUCUMBER	○ MANGO		
○ CABBAGE	○ BELL PEPPER	○ POTATO	○ LIME	○ HANDMADE	○ PRE-PACKAGED

OTHER	MEAT

SALSA TYPE			SPICE LEVEL				
○ PICO DE GALLO	○ VERDE	○ ROJA	○ 1	○ 2	○ 3	○ 4	○ 5
○ JALAPEÑO	○ GUACAMOLE	○ GUAJILLO	SERVICE				
○ CHIPOTLE	○ TAQUERIA STYLE	○ OTHER	○ 1	○ 2	○ 3	○ 4	○ 5

WOULD YOU GO BACK?		OVERALL RATING
○ YES	○ NO	/ 10

TACO LOGBOOK

DATE			○ DINE-IN	○ STREET
TACO SHOP				
LOCATION		COST	$	
TACO TYPE				

NOTES	CUISINE	
	○ MEXICAN	○ FUSION
	○ TEX-MEX	○ OTHER

TOPPINGS				TORTILLA	
○ RICE	○ TOMATO	○ AVOCADO	○ CORN	○ FLOUR	○ CORN
○ BEANS	○ ONION	○ CARROT	○ EGG	○ SOFT	○ HARD
○ CHEESE	○ CILANTRO	○ RADISH	○ OLIVE	○ OTHER	
○ LETTUCE	○ JALAPEÑO	○ CUCUMBER	○ MANGO		
○ CABBAGE	○ BELL PEPPER	○ POTATO	○ LIME	○ HANDMADE	○ PRE-PACKAGED

OTHER	MEAT

SALSA TYPE			SPICE LEVEL				
○ PICO DE GALLO	○ VERDE	○ ROJA	○ 1	○ 2	○ 3	○ 4	○ 5
○ JALAPEÑO	○ GUACAMOLE	○ GUAJILLO	SERVICE				
○ CHIPOTLE	○ TAQUERIA STYLE	○ OTHER	○ 1	○ 2	○ 3	○ 4	○ 5

WOULD YOU GO BACK?		OVERALL RATING
○ YES	○ NO	/ 10

TACO LOGBOOK

DATE			○ DINE-IN	○ STREET
TACO SHOP				
LOCATION		COST	$	
TACO TYPE				

NOTES		CUISINE	
		○ MEXICAN	○ FUSION
		○ TEX-MEX	○ OTHER

TOPPINGS				TORTILLA	
○ RICE	○ TOMATO	○ AVOCADO	○ CORN	○ FLOUR	○ CORN
○ BEANS	○ ONION	○ CARROT	○ EGG	○ SOFT	○ HARD
○ CHEESE	○ CILANTRO	○ RADISH	○ OLIVE	○ OTHER	
○ LETTUCE	○ JALAPEÑO	○ CUCUMBER	○ MANGO		
○ CABBAGE	○ BELL PEPPER	○ POTATO	○ LIME	○ HANDMADE	○ PRE-PACKAGED

OTHER	MEAT

SALSA TYPE			SPICE LEVEL				
○ PICO DE GALLO	○ VERDE	○ ROJA	○ 1	○ 2	○ 3	○ 4	○ 5
○ JALAPEÑO	○ GUACAMOLE	○ GUAJILLO	SERVICE				
○ CHIPOTLE	○ TAQUERIA STYLE	○ OTHER	○ 1	○ 2	○ 3	○ 4	○ 5

WOULD YOU GO BACK?		OVERALL RATING
○ YES	○ NO	/ 10

TACO LOGBOOK

DATE		○ DINE-IN	○ STREET
TACO SHOP			
LOCATION		COST	$
TACO TYPE			

NOTES	CUISINE	
	○ MEXICAN	○ FUSION
	○ TEX-MEX	○ OTHER

TOPPINGS				TORTILLA	
○ RICE	○ TOMATO	○ AVOCADO	○ CORN	○ FLOUR	○ CORN
○ BEANS	○ ONION	○ CARROT	○ EGG	○ SOFT	○ HARD
○ CHEESE	○ CILANTRO	○ RADISH	○ OLIVE	○ OTHER	
○ LETTUCE	○ JALAPEÑO	○ CUCUMBER	○ MANGO		
○ CABBAGE	○ BELL PEPPER	○ POTATO	○ LIME	○ HANDMADE	○ PRE-PACKAGED

OTHER	MEAT

SALSA TYPE			SPICE LEVEL				
○ PICO DE GALLO	○ VERDE	○ ROJA	○ 1	○ 2	○ 3	○ 4	○ 5
○ JALAPEÑO	○ GUACAMOLE	○ GUAJILLO	SERVICE				
○ CHIPOTLE	○ TAQUERIA STYLE	○ OTHER	○ 1	○ 2	○ 3	○ 4	○ 5

WOULD YOU GO BACK?		OVERALL RATING
○ YES	○ NO	/ 10

TACO LOGBOOK

DATE			○ DINE-IN	○ STREET
TACO SHOP				
LOCATION			COST	$
TACO TYPE				

NOTES	CUISINE	
	○ MEXICAN	○ FUSION
	○ TEX-MEX	○ OTHER

TOPPINGS				TORTILLA	
○ RICE	○ TOMATO	○ AVOCADO	○ CORN	○ FLOUR	○ CORN
○ BEANS	○ ONION	○ CARROT	○ EGG	○ SOFT	○ HARD
○ CHEESE	○ CILANTRO	○ RADISH	○ OLIVE	○ OTHER	
○ LETTUCE	○ JALAPEÑO	○ CUCUMBER	○ MANGO		
○ CABBAGE	○ BELL PEPPER	○ POTATO	○ LIME	○ HANDMADE	○ PRE-PACKAGED

OTHER	MEAT

SALSA TYPE			SPICE LEVEL				
○ PICO DE GALLO	○ VERDE	○ ROJA	○ 1	○ 2	○ 3	○ 4	○ 5
○ JALAPEÑO	○ GUACAMOLE	○ GUAJILLO	SERVICE				
○ CHIPOTLE	○ TAQUERIA STYLE	○ OTHER	○ 1	○ 2	○ 3	○ 4	○ 5

WOULD YOU GO BACK?		OVERALL RATING
○ YES	○ NO	/ 10

TACO LOGBOOK

DATE			○ DINE-IN	○ STREET
TACO SHOP				
LOCATION		COST	$	
TACO TYPE				

NOTES	CUISINE	
	○ MEXICAN	○ FUSION
	○ TEX-MEX	○ OTHER

TOPPINGS				TORTILLA	
○ RICE	○ TOMATO	○ AVOCADO	○ CORN	○ FLOUR	○ CORN
○ BEANS	○ ONION	○ CARROT	○ EGG	○ SOFT	○ HARD
○ CHEESE	○ CILANTRO	○ RADISH	○ OLIVE	○ OTHER	
○ LETTUCE	○ JALAPEÑO	○ CUCUMBER	○ MANGO		
○ CABBAGE	○ BELL PEPPER	○ POTATO	○ LIME	○ HANDMADE	○ PRE-PACKAGED

OTHER	MEAT

SALSA TYPE			SPICE LEVEL				
○ PICO DE GALLO	○ VERDE	○ ROJA	○ 1	○ 2	○ 3	○ 4	○ 5
○ JALAPEÑO	○ GUACAMOLE	○ GUAJILLO	SERVICE				
○ CHIPOTLE	○ TAQUERIA STYLE	○ OTHER	○ 1	○ 2	○ 3	○ 4	○ 5

WOULD YOU GO BACK?	OVERALL RATING
○ YES ○ NO	/ 10

TACO LOGBOOK

DATE			○ DINE-IN	○ STREET
TACO SHOP				
LOCATION		COST	$	
TACO TYPE				

NOTES	CUISINE	
	○ MEXICAN	○ FUSION
	○ TEX-MEX	○ OTHER

TOPPINGS				TORTILLA	
○ RICE	○ TOMATO	○ AVOCADO	○ CORN	○ FLOUR	○ CORN
○ BEANS	○ ONION	○ CARROT	○ EGG	○ SOFT	○ HARD
○ CHEESE	○ CILANTRO	○ RADISH	○ OLIVE	○ OTHER	
○ LETTUCE	○ JALAPEÑO	○ CUCUMBER	○ MANGO		
○ CABBAGE	○ BELL PEPPER	○ POTATO	○ LIME	○ HANDMADE	○ PRE-PACKAGED

OTHER	MEAT

SALSA TYPE			SPICE LEVEL				
○ PICO DE GALLO	○ VERDE	○ ROJA	○ 1	○ 2	○ 3	○ 4	○ 5
○ JALAPEÑO	○ GUACAMOLE	○ GUAJILLO	SERVICE				
○ CHIPOTLE	○ TAQUERIA STYLE	○ OTHER	○ 1	○ 2	○ 3	○ 4	○ 5

WOULD YOU GO BACK?		OVERALL RATING
○ YES	○ NO	/ 10

TACO LOGBOOK

DATE			○ DINE-IN	○ STREET
TACO SHOP				
LOCATION		COST	$	
TACO TYPE				

NOTES	CUISINE	
	○ MEXICAN	○ FUSION
	○ TEX-MEX	○ OTHER

TOPPINGS				TORTILLA	
○ RICE	○ TOMATO	○ AVOCADO	○ CORN	○ FLOUR	○ CORN
○ BEANS	○ ONION	○ CARROT	○ EGG	○ SOFT	○ HARD
○ CHEESE	○ CILANTRO	○ RADISH	○ OLIVE	○ OTHER	
○ LETTUCE	○ JALAPEÑO	○ CUCUMBER	○ MANGO		
○ CABBAGE	○ BELL PEPPER	○ POTATO	○ LIME	○ HANDMADE	○ PRE-PACKAGED

OTHER	MEAT

SALSA TYPE			SPICE LEVEL				
○ PICO DE GALLO	○ VERDE	○ ROJA	○ 1	○ 2	○ 3	○ 4	○ 5
○ JALAPEÑO	○ GUACAMOLE	○ GUAJILLO	SERVICE				
○ CHIPOTLE	○ TAQUERIA STYLE	○ OTHER	○ 1	○ 2	○ 3	○ 4	○ 5

WOULD YOU GO BACK?		OVERALL RATING
○ YES	○ NO	/ 10

TACO LOGBOOK

DATE			○ DINE-IN	○ STREET
TACO SHOP				
LOCATION		COST	$	
TACO TYPE				

NOTES	CUISINE	
	○ MEXICAN	○ FUSION
	○ TEX-MEX	○ OTHER

TOPPINGS | TORTILLA

○ RICE	○ TOMATO	○ AVOCADO	○ CORN	○ FLOUR	○ CORN
○ BEANS	○ ONION	○ CARROT	○ EGG	○ SOFT	○ HARD
○ CHEESE	○ CILANTRO	○ RADISH	○ OLIVE	○ OTHER	
○ LETTUCE	○ JALAPEÑO	○ CUCUMBER	○ MANGO		
○ CABBAGE	○ BELL PEPPER	○ POTATO	○ LIME	○ HANDMADE	○ PRE-PACKAGED

OTHER | MEAT

SALSA TYPE | SPICE LEVEL

○ PICO DE GALLO	○ VERDE	○ ROJA	○ 1	○ 2	○ 3	○ 4	○ 5
○ JALAPEÑO	○ GUACAMOLE	○ GUAJILLO	SERVICE				
○ CHIPOTLE	○ TAQUERIA STYLE	○ OTHER	○ 1	○ 2	○ 3	○ 4	○ 5

WOULD YOU GO BACK? | OVERALL RATING

○ YES	○ NO	/ 10

TACO LOGBOOK

DATE			○ DINE-IN	○ STREET
TACO SHOP				
LOCATION			COST	$
TACO TYPE				

NOTES	CUISINE	
	○ MEXICAN	○ FUSION
	○ TEX-MEX	○ OTHER

TOPPINGS				TORTILLA	
○ RICE	○ TOMATO	○ AVOCADO	○ CORN	○ FLOUR	○ CORN
○ BEANS	○ ONION	○ CARROT	○ EGG	○ SOFT	○ HARD
○ CHEESE	○ CILANTRO	○ RADISH	○ OLIVE	○ OTHER	
○ LETTUCE	○ JALAPEÑO	○ CUCUMBER	○ MANGO		
○ CABBAGE	○ BELL PEPPER	○ POTATO	○ LIME	○ HANDMADE	○ PRE-PACKAGED

OTHER	MEAT

SALSA TYPE			SPICE LEVEL				
○ PICO DE GALLO	○ VERDE	○ ROJA	○ 1	○ 2	○ 3	○ 4	○ 5
○ JALAPEÑO	○ GUACAMOLE	○ GUAJILLO	SERVICE				
○ CHIPOTLE	○ TAQUERIA STYLE	○ OTHER	○ 1	○ 2	○ 3	○ 4	○ 5

WOULD YOU GO BACK?		OVERALL RATING
○ YES	○ NO	/ 10

TACO LOGBOOK

DATE			○ DINE-IN	○ STREET
TACO SHOP				
LOCATION			COST	$
TACO TYPE				

NOTES		CUISINE	
		○ MEXICAN	○ FUSION
		○ TEX-MEX	○ OTHER

TOPPINGS				TORTILLA	
○ RICE	○ TOMATO	○ AVOCADO	○ CORN	○ FLOUR	○ CORN
○ BEANS	○ ONION	○ CARROT	○ EGG	○ SOFT	○ HARD
○ CHEESE	○ CILANTRO	○ RADISH	○ OLIVE	○ OTHER	
○ LETTUCE	○ JALAPEÑO	○ CUCUMBER	○ MANGO		
○ CABBAGE	○ BELL PEPPER	○ POTATO	○ LIME	○ HANDMADE	○ PRE-PACKAGED

OTHER	MEAT

SALSA TYPE			SPICE LEVEL				
○ PICO DE GALLO	○ VERDE	○ ROJA	○ 1	○ 2	○ 3	○ 4	○ 5
○ JALAPEÑO	○ GUACAMOLE	○ GUAJILLO	SERVICE				
○ CHIPOTLE	○ TAQUERIA STYLE	○ OTHER	○ 1	○ 2	○ 3	○ 4	○ 5

WOULD YOU GO BACK?		OVERALL RATING
○ YES	○ NO	/ 10

TACO LOGBOOK

DATE		○ DINE-IN	○ STREET
TACO SHOP			
LOCATION		COST	$
TACO TYPE			

NOTES

CUISINE

- ○ MEXICAN
- ○ FUSION
- ○ TEX-MEX
- ○ OTHER

TOPPINGS

○ RICE	○ TOMATO	○ AVOCADO	○ CORN
○ BEANS	○ ONION	○ CARROT	○ EGG
○ CHEESE	○ CILANTRO	○ RADISH	○ OLIVE
○ LETTUCE	○ JALAPEÑO	○ CUCUMBER	○ MANGO
○ CABBAGE	○ BELL PEPPER	○ POTATO	○ LIME

TORTILLA

○ FLOUR	○ CORN
○ SOFT	○ HARD
○ OTHER	
○ HANDMADE	○ PRE-PACKAGED

OTHER

MEAT

SALSA TYPE

○ PICO DE GALLO	○ VERDE	○ ROJA
○ JALAPEÑO	○ GUACAMOLE	○ GUAJILLO
○ CHIPOTLE	○ TAQUERIA STYLE	○ OTHER

SPICE LEVEL

○ 1   ○ 2   ○ 3   ○ 4   ○ 5

SERVICE

○ 1   ○ 2   ○ 3   ○ 4   ○ 5

WOULD YOU GO BACK?

○ YES   ○ NO

OVERALL RATING

/ 10

TACO LOGBOOK

DATE			○ DINE-IN	○ STREET
TACO SHOP				
LOCATION			COST	$
TACO TYPE				

NOTES	CUISINE	
	○ MEXICAN	○ FUSION
	○ TEX-MEX	○ OTHER

TOPPINGS				TORTILLA	
○ RICE	○ TOMATO	○ AVOCADO	○ CORN	○ FLOUR	○ CORN
○ BEANS	○ ONION	○ CARROT	○ EGG	○ SOFT	○ HARD
○ CHEESE	○ CILANTRO	○ RADISH	○ OLIVE	○ OTHER	
○ LETTUCE	○ JALAPEÑO	○ CUCUMBER	○ MANGO		
○ CABBAGE	○ BELL PEPPER	○ POTATO	○ LIME	○ HANDMADE	○ PRE-PACKAGED

OTHER	MEAT

SALSA TYPE			SPICE LEVEL				
○ PICO DE GALLO	○ VERDE	○ ROJA	○ 1	○ 2	○ 3	○ 4	○ 5
○ JALAPEÑO	○ GUACAMOLE	○ GUAJILLO	SERVICE				
○ CHIPOTLE	○ TAQUERIA STYLE	○ OTHER	○ 1	○ 2	○ 3	○ 4	○ 5

WOULD YOU GO BACK?		OVERALL RATING
○ YES	○ NO	/ 10

TACO LOGBOOK

DATE		○ DINE-IN	○ STREET
TACO SHOP			
LOCATION		COST $	
TACO TYPE			

NOTES	CUISINE	
	○ MEXICAN	○ FUSION
	○ TEX-MEX	○ OTHER

TOPPINGS				TORTILLA	
○ RICE	○ TOMATO	○ AVOCADO	○ CORN	○ FLOUR	○ CORN
○ BEANS	○ ONION	○ CARROT	○ EGG	○ SOFT	○ HARD
○ CHEESE	○ CILANTRO	○ RADISH	○ OLIVE	○ OTHER	
○ LETTUCE	○ JALAPEÑO	○ CUCUMBER	○ MANGO		
○ CABBAGE	○ BELL PEPPER	○ POTATO	○ LIME	○ HANDMADE	○ PRE-PACKAGED

OTHER	MEAT

SALSA TYPE			SPICE LEVEL				
○ PICO DE GALLO	○ VERDE	○ ROJA	○ 1	○ 2	○ 3	○ 4	○ 5
○ JALAPEÑO	○ GUACAMOLE	○ GUAJILLO	SERVICE				
○ CHIPOTLE	○ TAQUERIA STYLE	○ OTHER	○ 1	○ 2	○ 3	○ 4	○ 5

WOULD YOU GO BACK?		OVERALL RATING
○ YES	○ NO	/ 10

TACO LOGBOOK

DATE		○ DINE-IN	○ STREET
TACO SHOP			
LOCATION		**COST**	$
TACO TYPE			

NOTES	CUISINE	
	○ MEXICAN	○ FUSION
	○ TEX-MEX	○ OTHER

TOPPINGS				TORTILLA	
○ RICE	○ TOMATO	○ AVOCADO	○ CORN	○ FLOUR	○ CORN
○ BEANS	○ ONION	○ CARROT	○ EGG	○ SOFT	○ HARD
○ CHEESE	○ CILANTRO	○ RADISH	○ OLIVE	○ OTHER	
○ LETTUCE	○ JALAPEÑO	○ CUCUMBER	○ MANGO		
○ CABBAGE	○ BELL PEPPER	○ POTATO	○ LIME	○ HANDMADE	○ PRE-PACKAGED

OTHER	MEAT

SALSA TYPE			SPICE LEVEL				
○ PICO DE GALLO	○ VERDE	○ ROJA	○ 1	○ 2	○ 3	○ 4	○ 5
○ JALAPEÑO	○ GUACAMOLE	○ GUAJILLO	SERVICE				
○ CHIPOTLE	○ TAQUERIA STYLE	○ OTHER	○ 1	○ 2	○ 3	○ 4	○ 5

WOULD YOU GO BACK?		OVERALL RATING
○ YES	○ NO	/ 10

TACO LOGBOOK

DATE			○ DINE-IN	○ STREET
TACO SHOP				
LOCATION		COST	$	
TACO TYPE				

NOTES	CUISINE	
	○ MEXICAN	○ FUSION
	○ TEX-MEX	○ OTHER

TOPPINGS				TORTILLA	
○ RICE	○ TOMATO	○ AVOCADO	○ CORN	○ FLOUR	○ CORN
○ BEANS	○ ONION	○ CARROT	○ EGG	○ SOFT	○ HARD
○ CHEESE	○ CILANTRO	○ RADISH	○ OLIVE	○ OTHER	
○ LETTUCE	○ JALAPEÑO	○ CUCUMBER	○ MANGO		
○ CABBAGE	○ BELL PEPPER	○ POTATO	○ LIME	○ HANDMADE	○ PRE-PACKAGED

OTHER	MEAT

SALSA TYPE			SPICE LEVEL				
○ PICO DE GALLO	○ VERDE	○ ROJA	○ 1	○ 2	○ 3	○ 4	○ 5
○ JALAPEÑO	○ GUACAMOLE	○ GUAJILLO	SERVICE				
○ CHIPOTLE	○ TAQUERIA STYLE	○ OTHER	○ 1	○ 2	○ 3	○ 4	○ 5

WOULD YOU GO BACK?		OVERALL RATING
○ YES	○ NO	/ 10

TACO LOGBOOK

DATE			○ DINE-IN	○ STREET
TACO SHOP				
LOCATION		COST	$	
TACO TYPE				

NOTES	CUISINE	
	○ MEXICAN	○ FUSION
	○ TEX-MEX	○ OTHER

TOPPINGS				TORTILLA	
○ RICE	○ TOMATO	○ AVOCADO	○ CORN	○ FLOUR	○ CORN
○ BEANS	○ ONION	○ CARROT	○ EGG	○ SOFT	○ HARD
○ CHEESE	○ CILANTRO	○ RADISH	○ OLIVE	○ OTHER	
○ LETTUCE	○ JALAPEÑO	○ CUCUMBER	○ MANGO		
○ CABBAGE	○ BELL PEPPER	○ POTATO	○ LIME	○ HANDMADE	○ PRE-PACKAGED

OTHER	MEAT

SALSA TYPE			SPICE LEVEL				
○ PICO DE GALLO	○ VERDE	○ ROJA	○ 1	○ 2	○ 3	○ 4	○ 5
○ JALAPEÑO	○ GUACAMOLE	○ GUAJILLO	SERVICE				
○ CHIPOTLE	○ TAQUERIA STYLE	○ OTHER	○ 1	○ 2	○ 3	○ 4	○ 5

WOULD YOU GO BACK?		OVERALL RATING
○ YES	○ NO	/ 10

TACO LOGBOOK

DATE			○ DINE-IN	○ STREET
TACO SHOP				
LOCATION		COST	$	
TACO TYPE				

NOTES	CUISINE	
	○ MEXICAN	○ FUSION
	○ TEX-MEX	○ OTHER

TOPPINGS				TORTILLA	
○ RICE	○ TOMATO	○ AVOCADO	○ CORN	○ FLOUR	○ CORN
○ BEANS	○ ONION	○ CARROT	○ EGG	○ SOFT	○ HARD
○ CHEESE	○ CILANTRO	○ RADISH	○ OLIVE	○ OTHER	
○ LETTUCE	○ JALAPEÑO	○ CUCUMBER	○ MANGO		
○ CABBAGE	○ BELL PEPPER	○ POTATO	○ LIME	○ HANDMADE	○ PRE-PACKAGED

OTHER	MEAT

SALSA TYPE			SPICE LEVEL				
○ PICO DE GALLO	○ VERDE	○ ROJA	○ 1	○ 2	○ 3	○ 4	○ 5
○ JALAPEÑO	○ GUACAMOLE	○ GUAJILLO	SERVICE				
○ CHIPOTLE	○ TAQUERIA STYLE	○ OTHER	○ 1	○ 2	○ 3	○ 4	○ 5

WOULD YOU GO BACK?	OVERALL RATING
○ YES ○ NO	/ 10

TACO LOGBOOK

DATE			○ DINE-IN	○ STREET
TACO SHOP				
LOCATION			COST	$
TACO TYPE				

NOTES		CUISINE	
		○ MEXICAN	○ FUSION
		○ TEX-MEX	○ OTHER

TOPPINGS				TORTILLA	
○ RICE	○ TOMATO	○ AVOCADO	○ CORN	○ FLOUR	○ CORN
○ BEANS	○ ONION	○ CARROT	○ EGG	○ SOFT	○ HARD
○ CHEESE	○ CILANTRO	○ RADISH	○ OLIVE	○ OTHER	
○ LETTUCE	○ JALAPEÑO	○ CUCUMBER	○ MANGO		
○ CABBAGE	○ BELL PEPPER	○ POTATO	○ LIME	○ HANDMADE	○ PRE-PACKAGED

OTHER	MEAT

SALSA TYPE			SPICE LEVEL				
○ PICO DE GALLO	○ VERDE	○ ROJA	○ 1	○ 2	○ 3	○ 4	○ 5
○ JALAPEÑO	○ GUACAMOLE	○ GUAJILLO	SERVICE				
○ CHIPOTLE	○ TAQUERIA STYLE	○ OTHER	○ 1	○ 2	○ 3	○ 4	○ 5

WOULD YOU GO BACK?		OVERALL RATING
○ YES	○ NO	/ 10

TACO LOGBOOK

DATE			○ DINE-IN	○ STREET
TACO SHOP				
LOCATION		COST $		
TACO TYPE				

NOTES	CUISINE	
	○ MEXICAN	○ FUSION
	○ TEX-MEX	○ OTHER

TOPPINGS				TORTILLA	
○ RICE	○ TOMATO	○ AVOCADO	○ CORN	○ FLOUR	○ CORN
○ BEANS	○ ONION	○ CARROT	○ EGG	○ SOFT	○ HARD
○ CHEESE	○ CILANTRO	○ RADISH	○ OLIVE	○ OTHER	
○ LETTUCE	○ JALAPEÑO	○ CUCUMBER	○ MANGO		
○ CABBAGE	○ BELL PEPPER	○ POTATO	○ LIME	○ HANDMADE	○ PRE-PACKAGED

OTHER	MEAT

SALSA TYPE			SPICE LEVEL				
○ PICO DE GALLO	○ VERDE	○ ROJA	○ 1	○ 2	○ 3	○ 4	○ 5
○ JALAPEÑO	○ GUACAMOLE	○ GUAJILLO	SERVICE				
○ CHIPOTLE	○ TAQUERIA STYLE	○ OTHER	○ 1	○ 2	○ 3	○ 4	○ 5

WOULD YOU GO BACK?		OVERALL RATING
○ YES	○ NO	/ 10

TACO LOGBOOK

DATE			○ DINE-IN	○ STREET
TACO SHOP				
LOCATION		COST	$	
TACO TYPE				

NOTES	CUISINE	
	○ MEXICAN	○ FUSION
	○ TEX-MEX	○ OTHER

TOPPINGS				TORTILLA	
○ RICE	○ TOMATO	○ AVOCADO	○ CORN	○ FLOUR	○ CORN
○ BEANS	○ ONION	○ CARROT	○ EGG	○ SOFT	○ HARD
○ CHEESE	○ CILANTRO	○ RADISH	○ OLIVE	○ OTHER	
○ LETTUCE	○ JALAPEÑO	○ CUCUMBER	○ MANGO		
○ CABBAGE	○ BELL PEPPER	○ POTATO	○ LIME	○ HANDMADE	○ PRE-PACKAGED

OTHER	MEAT

SALSA TYPE			SPICE LEVEL				
○ PICO DE GALLO	○ VERDE	○ ROJA	○ 1	○ 2	○ 3	○ 4	○ 5
○ JALAPEÑO	○ GUACAMOLE	○ GUAJILLO	SERVICE				
○ CHIPOTLE	○ TAQUERIA STYLE	○ OTHER	○ 1	○ 2	○ 3	○ 4	○ 5

WOULD YOU GO BACK?		OVERALL RATING
○ YES	○ NO	/ 10

TACO LOGBOOK

DATE				○ DINE-IN	○ STREET
TACO SHOP					
LOCATION				COST	$
TACO TYPE					

NOTES				CUISINE	
				○ MEXICAN	○ FUSION
				○ TEX-MEX	○ OTHER

TOPPINGS				TORTILLA	
○ RICE	○ TOMATO	○ AVOCADO	○ CORN	○ FLOUR	○ CORN
○ BEANS	○ ONION	○ CARROT	○ EGG	○ SOFT	○ HARD
○ CHEESE	○ CILANTRO	○ RADISH	○ OLIVE	○ OTHER	
○ LETTUCE	○ JALAPEÑO	○ CUCUMBER	○ MANGO		
○ CABBAGE	○ BELL PEPPER	○ POTATO	○ LIME	○ HANDMADE	○ PRE-PACKAGED

OTHER			MEAT	

SALSA TYPE			SPICE LEVEL				
○ PICO DE GALLO	○ VERDE	○ ROJA	○ 1	○ 2	○ 3	○ 4	○ 5
○ JALAPEÑO	○ GUACAMOLE	○ GUAJILLO	SERVICE				
○ CHIPOTLE	○ TAQUERIA STYLE	○ OTHER	○ 1	○ 2	○ 3	○ 4	○ 5

WOULD YOU GO BACK?		OVERALL RATING
○ YES	○ NO	/ 10

TACO LOGBOOK

DATE			○ DINE-IN	○ STREET
TACO SHOP				
LOCATION			COST	$
TACO TYPE				

NOTES	CUISINE	
	○ MEXICAN	○ FUSION
	○ TEX-MEX	○ OTHER

TOPPINGS				TORTILLA	
○ RICE	○ TOMATO	○ AVOCADO	○ CORN	○ FLOUR	○ CORN
○ BEANS	○ ONION	○ CARROT	○ EGG	○ SOFT	○ HARD
○ CHEESE	○ CILANTRO	○ RADISH	○ OLIVE	○ OTHER	
○ LETTUCE	○ JALAPEÑO	○ CUCUMBER	○ MANGO		
○ CABBAGE	○ BELL PEPPER	○ POTATO	○ LIME	○ HANDMADE	○ PRE-PACKAGED

OTHER	MEAT

SALSA TYPE			SPICE LEVEL				
○ PICO DE GALLO	○ VERDE	○ ROJA	○ 1	○ 2	○ 3	○ 4	○ 5
○ JALAPEÑO	○ GUACAMOLE	○ GUAJILLO	SERVICE				
○ CHIPOTLE	○ TAQUERIA STYLE	○ OTHER	○ 1	○ 2	○ 3	○ 4	○ 5

WOULD YOU GO BACK?		OVERALL RATING
○ YES	○ NO	/ 10

TACO LOGBOOK

DATE			○ DINE-IN	○ STREET
TACO SHOP				
LOCATION		COST	$	
TACO TYPE				

NOTES		CUISINE	
		○ MEXICAN	○ FUSION
		○ TEX-MEX	○ OTHER

TOPPINGS				TORTILLA	
○ RICE	○ TOMATO	○ AVOCADO	○ CORN	○ FLOUR	○ CORN
○ BEANS	○ ONION	○ CARROT	○ EGG	○ SOFT	○ HARD
○ CHEESE	○ CILANTRO	○ RADISH	○ OLIVE	○ OTHER	
○ LETTUCE	○ JALAPEÑO	○ CUCUMBER	○ MANGO		
○ CABBAGE	○ BELL PEPPER	○ POTATO	○ LIME	○ HANDMADE	○ PRE-PACKAGED

OTHER	MEAT

SALSA TYPE			SPICE LEVEL				
○ PICO DE GALLO	○ VERDE	○ ROJA	○ 1	○ 2	○ 3	○ 4	○ 5
○ JALAPEÑO	○ GUACAMOLE	○ GUAJILLO	SERVICE				
○ CHIPOTLE	○ TAQUERIA STYLE	○ OTHER	○ 1	○ 2	○ 3	○ 4	○ 5

WOULD YOU GO BACK?		OVERALL RATING
○ YES	○ NO	/ 10

TACO LOGBOOK

DATE			○ DINE-IN	○ STREET
TACO SHOP				
LOCATION		COST	$	
TACO TYPE				

NOTES	CUISINE	
	○ MEXICAN	○ FUSION
	○ TEX-MEX	○ OTHER

TOPPINGS				TORTILLA	
○ RICE	○ TOMATO	○ AVOCADO	○ CORN	○ FLOUR	○ CORN
○ BEANS	○ ONION	○ CARROT	○ EGG	○ SOFT	○ HARD
○ CHEESE	○ CILANTRO	○ RADISH	○ OLIVE	○ OTHER	
○ LETTUCE	○ JALAPEÑO	○ CUCUMBER	○ MANGO		
○ CABBAGE	○ BELL PEPPER	○ POTATO	○ LIME	○ HANDMADE	○ PRE-PACKAGED

OTHER	MEAT

SALSA TYPE			SPICE LEVEL				
○ PICO DE GALLO	○ VERDE	○ ROJA	○ 1	○ 2	○ 3	○ 4	○ 5
○ JALAPEÑO	○ GUACAMOLE	○ GUAJILLO	SERVICE				
○ CHIPOTLE	○ TAQUERIA STYLE	○ OTHER	○ 1	○ 2	○ 3	○ 4	○ 5

WOULD YOU GO BACK?		OVERALL RATING
○ YES	○ NO	/ 10

TACO LOGBOOK

DATE			○ DINE-IN	○ STREET
TACO SHOP				
LOCATION		COST	$	
TACO TYPE				

NOTES	CUISINE	
	○ MEXICAN	○ FUSION
	○ TEX-MEX	○ OTHER

TOPPINGS				TORTILLA	
○ RICE	○ TOMATO	○ AVOCADO	○ CORN	○ FLOUR	○ CORN
○ BEANS	○ ONION	○ CARROT	○ EGG	○ SOFT	○ HARD
○ CHEESE	○ CILANTRO	○ RADISH	○ OLIVE	○ OTHER	
○ LETTUCE	○ JALAPEÑO	○ CUCUMBER	○ MANGO		
○ CABBAGE	○ BELL PEPPER	○ POTATO	○ LIME	○ HANDMADE	○ PRE-PACKAGED

OTHER	MEAT

SALSA TYPE			SPICE LEVEL				
○ PICO DE GALLO	○ VERDE	○ ROJA	○ 1	○ 2	○ 3	○ 4	○ 5
○ JALAPEÑO	○ GUACAMOLE	○ GUAJILLO	SERVICE				
○ CHIPOTLE	○ TAQUERIA STYLE	○ OTHER	○ 1	○ 2	○ 3	○ 4	○ 5

WOULD YOU GO BACK?		OVERALL RATING
○ YES	○ NO	/ 10

TACO LOGBOOK

DATE			○ DINE-IN	○ STREET
TACO SHOP				
LOCATION		COST	$	
TACO TYPE				

NOTES	CUISINE	
	○ MEXICAN	○ FUSION
	○ TEX-MEX	○ OTHER

TOPPINGS				TORTILLA	
○ RICE	○ TOMATO	○ AVOCADO	○ CORN	○ FLOUR	○ CORN
○ BEANS	○ ONION	○ CARROT	○ EGG	○ SOFT	○ HARD
○ CHEESE	○ CILANTRO	○ RADISH	○ OLIVE	○ OTHER	
○ LETTUCE	○ JALAPEÑO	○ CUCUMBER	○ MANGO		
○ CABBAGE	○ BELL PEPPER	○ POTATO	○ LIME	○ HANDMADE	○ PRE-PACKAGED

OTHER	MEAT

SALSA TYPE			SPICE LEVEL				
○ PICO DE GALLO	○ VERDE	○ ROJA	○ 1	○ 2	○ 3	○ 4	○ 5
○ JALAPEÑO	○ GUACAMOLE	○ GUAJILLO	SERVICE				
○ CHIPOTLE	○ TAQUERIA STYLE	○ OTHER	○ 1	○ 2	○ 3	○ 4	○ 5

WOULD YOU GO BACK?		OVERALL RATING
○ YES	○ NO	/ 10

TACO LOGBOOK

DATE			○ DINE-IN	○ STREET
TACO SHOP				
LOCATION		COST	$	
TACO TYPE				

NOTES	CUISINE	
	○ MEXICAN	○ FUSION
	○ TEX-MEX	○ OTHER

TOPPINGS

				TORTILLA	
○ RICE	○ TOMATO	○ AVOCADO	○ CORN	○ FLOUR	○ CORN
○ BEANS	○ ONION	○ CARROT	○ EGG	○ SOFT	○ HARD
○ CHEESE	○ CILANTRO	○ RADISH	○ OLIVE	○ OTHER	
○ LETTUCE	○ JALAPEÑO	○ CUCUMBER	○ MANGO		
○ CABBAGE	○ BELL PEPPER	○ POTATO	○ LIME	○ HANDMADE	○ PRE-PACKAGED

OTHER

MEAT

SALSA TYPE

			SPICE LEVEL				
○ PICO DE GALLO	○ VERDE	○ ROJA	○ 1	○ 2	○ 3	○ 4	○ 5
○ JALAPEÑO	○ GUACAMOLE	○ GUAJILLO	SERVICE				
○ CHIPOTLE	○ TAQUERIA STYLE	○ OTHER	○ 1	○ 2	○ 3	○ 4	○ 5

WOULD YOU GO BACK?	OVERALL RATING
○ YES ○ NO	/ 10

TACO LOGBOOK

DATE			○ DINE-IN	○ STREET
TACO SHOP				
LOCATION		COST	$	
TACO TYPE				

NOTES	CUISINE	
	○ MEXICAN	○ FUSION
	○ TEX-MEX	○ OTHER

TOPPINGS				TORTILLA	
○ RICE	○ TOMATO	○ AVOCADO	○ CORN	○ FLOUR	○ CORN
○ BEANS	○ ONION	○ CARROT	○ EGG	○ SOFT	○ HARD
○ CHEESE	○ CILANTRO	○ RADISH	○ OLIVE	○ OTHER	
○ LETTUCE	○ JALAPEÑO	○ CUCUMBER	○ MANGO		
○ CABBAGE	○ BELL PEPPER	○ POTATO	○ LIME	○ HANDMADE	○ PRE-PACKAGED

OTHER	MEAT

SALSA TYPE			SPICE LEVEL				
○ PICO DE GALLO	○ VERDE	○ ROJA	○ 1	○ 2	○ 3	○ 4	○ 5
○ JALAPEÑO	○ GUACAMOLE	○ GUAJILLO	SERVICE				
○ CHIPOTLE	○ TAQUERIA STYLE	○ OTHER	○ 1	○ 2	○ 3	○ 4	○ 5

WOULD YOU GO BACK?		OVERALL RATING
○ YES	○ NO	/ 10

TACO LOGBOOK

DATE			○ DINE-IN	○ STREET
TACO SHOP				
LOCATION		COST	$	
TACO TYPE				

NOTES	CUISINE	
	○ MEXICAN	○ FUSION
	○ TEX-MEX	○ OTHER

TOPPINGS				TORTILLA	
○ RICE	○ TOMATO	○ AVOCADO	○ CORN	○ FLOUR	○ CORN
○ BEANS	○ ONION	○ CARROT	○ EGG	○ SOFT	○ HARD
○ CHEESE	○ CILANTRO	○ RADISH	○ OLIVE	○ OTHER	
○ LETTUCE	○ JALAPEÑO	○ CUCUMBER	○ MANGO		
○ CABBAGE	○ BELL PEPPER	○ POTATO	○ LIME	○ HANDMADE	○ PRE-PACKAGED

OTHER	MEAT

SALSA TYPE			SPICE LEVEL				
○ PICO DE GALLO	○ VERDE	○ ROJA	○ 1	○ 2	○ 3	○ 4	○ 5
○ JALAPEÑO	○ GUACAMOLE	○ GUAJILLO	SERVICE				
○ CHIPOTLE	○ TAQUERIA STYLE	○ OTHER	○ 1	○ 2	○ 3	○ 4	○ 5

WOULD YOU GO BACK?		OVERALL RATING
○ YES	○ NO	/ 10

TACO LOGBOOK

DATE			○ DINE-IN	○ STREET
TACO SHOP				
LOCATION		COST	$	
TACO TYPE				

NOTES		CUISINE	
		○ MEXICAN	○ FUSION
		○ TEX-MEX	○ OTHER

TOPPINGS				TORTILLA	
○ RICE	○ TOMATO	○ AVOCADO	○ CORN	○ FLOUR	○ CORN
○ BEANS	○ ONION	○ CARROT	○ EGG	○ SOFT	○ HARD
○ CHEESE	○ CILANTRO	○ RADISH	○ OLIVE	○ OTHER	
○ LETTUCE	○ JALAPEÑO	○ CUCUMBER	○ MANGO		
○ CABBAGE	○ BELL PEPPER	○ POTATO	○ LIME	○ HANDMADE	○ PRE-PACKAGED

OTHER	MEAT

SALSA TYPE			SPICE LEVEL				
○ PICO DE GALLO	○ VERDE	○ ROJA	○ 1	○ 2	○ 3	○ 4	○ 5
○ JALAPEÑO	○ GUACAMOLE	○ GUAJILLO	SERVICE				
○ CHIPOTLE	○ TAQUERIA STYLE	○ OTHER	○ 1	○ 2	○ 3	○ 4	○ 5

WOULD YOU GO BACK?		OVERALL RATING
○ YES	○ NO	/ 10

TACO LOGBOOK

DATE		○ DINE-IN	○ STREET
TACO SHOP			
LOCATION		COST	$
TACO TYPE			

NOTES		CUISINE	
		○ MEXICAN	○ FUSION
		○ TEX-MEX	○ OTHER

TOPPINGS				TORTILLA	
○ RICE	○ TOMATO	○ AVOCADO	○ CORN	○ FLOUR	○ CORN
○ BEANS	○ ONION	○ CARROT	○ EGG	○ SOFT	○ HARD
○ CHEESE	○ CILANTRO	○ RADISH	○ OLIVE	○ OTHER	
○ LETTUCE	○ JALAPEÑO	○ CUCUMBER	○ MANGO		
○ CABBAGE	○ BELL PEPPER	○ POTATO	○ LIME	○ HANDMADE	○ PRE-PACKAGED

OTHER	MEAT

SALSA TYPE			SPICE LEVEL				
○ PICO DE GALLO	○ VERDE	○ ROJA	○ 1	○ 2	○ 3	○ 4	○ 5
○ JALAPEÑO	○ GUACAMOLE	○ GUAJILLO	SERVICE				
○ CHIPOTLE	○ TAQUERIA STYLE	○ OTHER	○ 1	○ 2	○ 3	○ 4	○ 5

WOULD YOU GO BACK?		OVERALL RATING
○ YES	○ NO	/ 10

www.ingramcontent.com/pod-product-compliance
Lightning Source LLC
Chambersburg PA
CBHW071408080526
44587CB00017B/3210